SHAKING THE NATIONS

Shaking the Nations

CLIFFORD HILL

KINGSWAY PUBLICATIONS
EASTBOURNE

First published 1995

ISBN 0 85476 575 1

Produced by Bookprint Creative Services
P.O. Box 827, BN21 3YJ, England, for
KINGSWAY PUBLICATIONS LTD
Lottbridge Drove, Eastbourne, E Sussex BN23 6NT.
Printed in Great Britain.

Contents

1

Change and Decay

Change and decay in all around I see,
O Thou who changest not abide with me.
Abide with me, Francis Lyte

'Got any change, guv?' The girl sitting on the steps of a central London church stretched out a grimy hand towards the approaching footsteps without even raising her head to look at her possible benefactor. Her face was unwashed and her hair matted. She looked thin and ill and although she was probably not yet twenty-five she looked much older as the combination of drugs and living rough left its mark. She is one of a growing army of homeless and hopeless young people to be found on the city streets of almost every nation in the western world. They are the rootless ones who see themselves as casualties of the system, victims of an unjust society in which they have no hope of succeeding—a society which holds no place for them and that they have rejected as firmly as they have been rejected.

Michael is thirty-eight, unmarried and still living with his parents. He has been unemployed for seven years. He has lost count of the number of job interviews he has attended but now there is a difference. When he applies for a job he no longer hopes he will get it but actually hopes he won't. He has lost all confidence in his ability to do a job. He feels unemployable. Lacking in self-esteem, he feels useless and worthless. Michael is just one of millions of long-term unemployed who have lost all sense of purpose in life, who look to the future without hope and for whom tomorrow is as empty as today.

These are just two small real-life pictures of human tragedy which are all too familiar in the western world of the 1990s. They illustrate the sense of hopelessness of those who feel trapped in a microcosm of poverty and deprivation in the midst of a world of affluence. It is a world which they can see all around them but which they are unable to enter. They can see the fruit of prosperity but they are unable to taste it. They have given up the unequal struggle; but there are millions more who continue to struggle while sharing in the growing sense of disillusionment with the whole materialistic and acquisitive basis of western society.

The economic problems of the 1990s which burst the bubble of prosperity enjoyed by the rich industrialised nations in the 1980s, are not the only causes of disillusionment in the West. Their roots are complex and are the result of a century of the most rapid and radical change in the entire history of mankind. These changes have transformed every aspect and area of life and all classes of society. Rich and poor alike, no one has remained untouched by the changes in technology, in political, economic and social life in the western world.

These radical changes which have transformed the whole of life throughout the twentieth century have had a deeply disturbing and unsettling effect upon countless millions of people in their private lives and their personal relationships as well as in the social spheres of life. A national survey in Britain in 1994, carried out for the JIM evangelistic campaign, revealed that the three words reflecting the attitudes of the majority of the British public were *fear*, *loneliness* and *despair*. This survey reveals not only a very serious social situation indicating a high level of social instability, but also immense personal insecurity and anxiety at an individual level and inevitably a high level of personal relationship problems affecting family and community life.

Before undertaking any more detailed analyses of these problems affecting both individuals and society as a whole it will be most helpful if we look at the causes rather than the symptoms. There is abundant evidence to show that a vast majority of people in the industrialised nations live under the constant pressures of stress. This occurs at all levels of society; among professionals as well as skilled and unskilled workers; among the rich and the poor. In fact it would probably be true to say that levels of stress have never been higher among those normally regarded as the privileged classes in society. The reasons for this we shall look at in more detail later. At this stage we are simply noting, by way of introduction, the existence of high levels of stresses and strains throughout the western industrialised nations.

In the less industrialised and developing nations social problems are of a different nature, being much more orientated to basic survival. The plain facts are that two-thirds of the world's population go to bed hungry at night. Millions face early death through famine, hunger, poverty, disease, the natural disasters of drought, flood and plague, plus the perennial problems of vast numbers of refugees created by war, fleeing from tribal conflict, political or social upheavals as well as natural disasters.

The global picture of a world in conflict and turmoil is not an exaggeration; it is reflected in daily news bulletins. The fictional horror generated by Hollywood films has been overtaken by reality. Today one often needs a strong constitution to sit and watch the daily television news transmissions. They reflect a level of cruelty and human suffering unique to our times. Of course it may be argued that there never were gentler days. Each generation tends to have its golden age myths set in the past. But it is undeniable that with the vast increase in world population during the twentieth century, the application of sophisticated technology to weapons of destruction, plus the high level of revolutionary political, economic and social change experienced during the second half of the century, a unique situation has been created in which every nation of the world is experiencing its own peculiar form of trauma. Due to the advances in global communications, international mobility and inter-dependence, no nation is an island. Each affects the other and contributes to a global picture of a world in turmoil.

The fear, loneliness and despair highlighted in the British social survey are probably fairly representative of social attitudes in many of the industrialised western nations where affluent lifestyles and job security are giving way to long-term unemployment.

Fear represents reaction to the growing level of violent crime and social disorder in all the western nations. This fear is increased by the media coverage of violence and the increasing level of activity among terrorists and their ability to catch the world headlines with a variety of atrocities and spectacular incidents. The fear of international terrorism has increased during the 1990s with the evidence of smuggled plutonium leaving Russia in the hands of international criminals. Supplies of enriched uranium and plutonium stored in various States of the former Soviet Union have been sold by disaffected scientists, technicians and officials. They once occupied privileged positions but in the aftermath of the demise of Communism and the resultant widespread social breakdown they see themselves as victims of the crumbling military industrial complex.

Loneliness has long been recognised as a characteristic of the social effects of the twin forces of urbanisation and industrialisation. Together they produce what the sociologist recognises as social *anomie*—a sense of isolation and alienation from society due to the depersonalising effects of an urban industrial environment in which the individual has little personal significance. It is very easy to be lonely in a crowd. Most city dwellers do not know even their immediate neighbours. They live independent lives and have little or no contact even with members of their own extended family. Indeed the extended family, characteristic of non-industrial societies and of the western nations a hundred years ago, today hardly exists in the West as a recognisable social unit. Many extended families only meet for weddings or funerals, which is a reflection of the rapid and radical social changes which have occurred during the twentieth century. One of the by-products of this is the loneliness of the individual and the lack of support experienced by people of all ages facing times of personal crisis.

Despair is often the result of inadequate support during times of crisis. The increasing level of suicide in the western nations is an indicator of a deep social malaise affecting personal security. The combined effects of the impact of social change upon individual lives, plus the perceived instability of the global situation and international issues for which there are apparently no solutions and no indications that things might get better, all combine to produce a sense of despair among millions of people who are unable to look to the future with any degree of hope.

This sounds a very depressing picture yet it is a realistic assessment of the international scene in the closing years of the second millennium. If we are to offer any hope for the future we have to begin by facing the facts, however daunting and unpleasant they may be. A realistic assessment of the situation is essential for creative change either at a corporate or an individual level. There has to be a realistic facing of the facts before creative policies of change can be introduced. This is true both for the individual and for society as a whole.

There are four major causal factors which can be discerned in accounting for the present global situation. These are largely applicable to the western industrialised nations, although to a lesser degree they also apply to other parts of the world, especially the states of the former Soviet Union. They are:

(1) De facto change
(2) Rate of change
(3) Philosophical concepts
(4) Historical factors

Each of these will be treated in some detail at a later stage but for the sake of clarity we will just add a few notes under each of these headings.

(1) De facto change

The older generation who have lived through most of the twentieth century have experienced revolutionary changes which have transformed the whole of life. In terms of social organisation Britain and most European states have moved, during the twentieth century, from a feudal-type, religiously sanctified, social organisation to a modern, secular democracy.

At the beginning of the century social status was ascribed at birth by position within the family and the family's position within society. There was very little social mobility, so people usually remained in the socio-economic class into which they were born. Today we live in an achievement-based society where qualifications and ability to compete are of prime importance. The technological and economic changes have revolutionised life for the entire population, bringing a high level of communications and mobility and an endless variety of opportunity, both for occupations and leisure activities. Political changes have had a revolutionary effect upon social order and the process of secularisation has transformed the beliefs, moral standards and social values of millions of people. These changes have combined to create, in a single century, a total transformation from the old stable world that had lasted for hundreds of years.

(2) Rate of change

The rate of change has been so fast that it has had a devastating effect upon the stability both of the individual and of society as a whole. The normal evolutionary rate of change through scientific invention and industrial development has been vastly accelerated during the twentieth century by two world wars. Thus the rate of change has not increased at a gentle uniform pace but has actually accelerated along an exponential curve. It is this increasing rate of change throughout the century which has resulted in a high level of personal and social instability. When everything around you is changing at a bewildering rate, and there are no fixed points of reference, everything in life can appear threatening. This can warp one's entire outlook upon life and create resistance to change, fear of the unknown and a sense of powerlessness—being driven by unseen forces over which the individual (or indeed whole nations) has no control. It is the accelerating rate of change through each decade of the twentieth century which has created the unstable world situation which we have today in which there appear to be no absolutes, no firmly fixed standards of behaviour. This in turn generates a lack of trust and affects personal relationships at all levels and increases fear and the sense of hopelessness.

(3) Philosophical concepts

The worldwide political, social and economic changes that have occurred during the twentieth century have resulted in fundamental conceptual changes in the value system underlying each of the nations. The value system in each nation is the product of its heritage, its social history, interwoven with, and to a certain extent moulded by, its religious and moral precepts. This value system is a major determinant of national characteristics. It is also of considerable social significance in contributing to the stability of a nation. In this sense the social value system functions as the foundations of the society and provides a yardstick for measuring the value of any proposed changes that affect the national way of life. For example, the British Sunday was, until the 1990s, protected from exploitation by commercialism. This ensured not only that people had the freedom to attend a place of worship but also could spend time with their families or in leisure pursuits of their choice. It was a day different from the rest of the week which had become part of the British way of life for a century or more. These protections, reinforced by both custom and legal constraints, were gradually eroded by the flouting of the law and then removed by legislation through the Sunday Trading Act of 1994.

A more dramatic example of change in philosophical concepts revolutionising the national way of life was provided by the collapse of Communism in the Soviet Union in 1990. The fundamental political change from a single party totalitarian system of government to an embryonic democracy, and a fundamental economic change from a centrally directed unified economy to a primitive free market economy, resulted in revolutionary changes to the entire social structure. This in turn brought to the surface a whole range of social values which had been suppressed for seventy years, such as nationalism within each of the member States, religious beliefs, freedom of speech, and a wide range of individually motivated ideas and ambitions which threatened both the well-being and the stability of every constituent part of the CIS.

What has happened in the former Soviet Union where there has been a massive rise in lawlessness, crime of all types, including large-scale organised Mafia-type operations, is a vivid illustration of the effects of rapid social change. Where this occurs with revolutionary speed the underlying value structure of the nation crumbles, which has the effect of destroying the foundational stability of that nation. To a greater or lesser extent this is what has happened in many nations throughout the world during the second half of the twentieth century. This can be seen among the rich nations and the poor, the industrialised and the developing nations, large and small, east and west, old established European nations, North America, Central and South America, newly emerging African nations both large and small from Algeria to South Africa; every nation in the Middle East and in the Far East from China to Indonesia. The social history of each nation could be taken as an example of fundamental changes affecting their underlying value systems, thereby shaking the foundations of each of the nations.

(4) Historical factors

It is easy to illustrate the twentieth century as a century of change. It can also be demonstrated that the rate of change has accelerated throughout the century with the consequent shaking of the foundations of the nations and the creation of a highly volatile international situation of great uncertainty and instability. One of the historical factors in this international trend is the almost unconscious recognition that we are in the last days of the second millennium. What this exactly means nobody can know for sure, but undoubtedly it does create an atmosphere of uncertainty and a lack of future predictability. It is in this context that the New Age movement has arisen, heralding a sea-change in social values. The New Age movement burst on the public scene in 1975 with an announcement that the Matreya or the 'Christ of all religions' was now in the world and that the end of the century would coincide with a new spiritual movement. This would mark the end of the age of Aries and the beginning of the age of Aquarius, which would result in a paradigm shift in the spiritual value system of the nations.

Undoubtedly the forces of secularism and secularisation have had a revolutionary effect upon spiritual values throughout the western world, which have had a particular impact upon the nations of Europe with their centuries of Christian tradition. The spiritual vacuum created by the loss of faith experienced by millions of Christians during the twentieth century has been compounded by population mobility and ease of communications which has brought a mixing of religions and strong drives towards inter-faith. This in turn has reinforced the New Age movement's objective of a one-world religion. Christians have seen this and its historical link with the approaching end of the second millennium as an indication that we are living in the last days of the present age. The expectation of divine intervention at a particular point in history in the not-too-distant future has increased among evangelical Christians in the closing decades of the twentieth century. Thus historical factors have combined with the changes experienced throughout the past century to increase the instability and volatility of the world situation.

The century of rapid change which has shaken the foundations of the nations has not only created a situation in which all the old certainties have disappeared, but has resulted in enormous instability both at an individual and a corporate level. One way of looking at this is in terms of goal frustration, that is, at the point where, on a personal or corporate level, our hopes, ambitions and desires are blocked. We all experience blocked goals in one way or another. How we react to such situations is a major determinant of our attitudes to life and of our social actions. Overleaf is a model of human reaction to blocked goals, or 'goal frustration'.

The reaction to finding our hopes and ambitions blocked may be either *positive* or *negative*, and under each of those headings it may be either *active* or *passive*. This model is a representation of the way either individuals or whole nations may react to such experience. This is a useful way of looking at our reactions and assessing the way we respond to such situations. The most positive and fruitful reaction to goal frustration is by actively engaging in lateral thinking and discovering alternative means of achieving the desired goal; or by the selection of an alternative goal which requires a fresh strategy for its implementation. The extreme negative reaction to goal frustration can result in total social inactivity or even suicide.

The national character of nations can be assessed through the use of this model as corporate human behaviour may follow similar lines. During the twentieth century we have seen whole nations turn to international

(1) POSITIVE REACTION

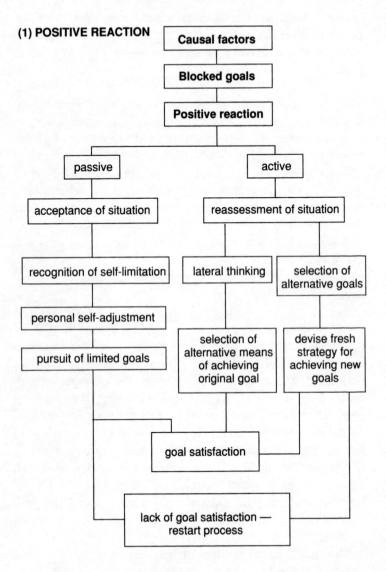

Model of human reactions to goal frustration

(2) NEGATIVE REACTION

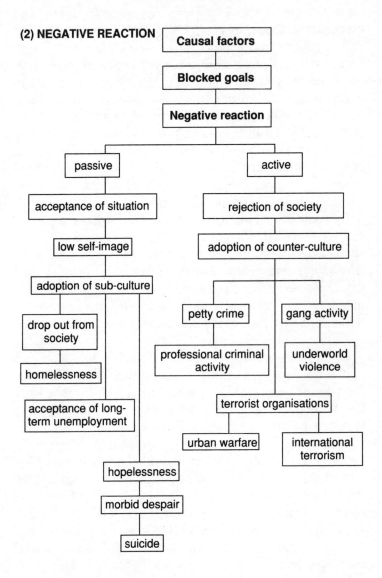

Model of human reactions to goal frustration

terrorism. Nations such as Germany, under the Nazis, and more recently Iran, Iraq and Libya have been notorious in this respect. Small nations in the developing world have accepted their limitations and inability to compete at all levels on the international scene and have thus chosen to adjust their national ambitions and pursue limited goals. Meanwhile other nations such as Germany and Japan, following defeat in the Second World War, have actively engaged in lateral thinking and selected alternative means of pursuing their original goals of the achievement of world power. This they have done through the exercise of industrial and economic development rather than military might.

By contrast, Britain has tended to go down the negative, passive, low self-image track, leading to less and less social activity on the international scene as first the British Empire disappeared into the pages of history and then the Commonwealth rapidly declined in international significance. The British public is still striving to come to terms with the loss of international power, prestige and pride.

One of the strange anomalies of history in the second half of the twentieth century is the way in which the hopes for a brave new world of peace and prosperity following the Second World War gradually evaporated and were replaced by the mood of pessimism which assailed the world in the 1990s. It is the contention which will be developed in later chapters that this transformation is due to the lack of firmly based social values underlying the nations in the western industrialised world. They have thereby been unable to exercise the moral and spiritual leadership in international affairs that traditionally has been expected of them and should have accompanied their economic and political power in the world.

It will further be contended that a major reason for this lack of moral and spiritual leadership has to be due to the declining influence of the church in the western nations. The church has been unable to give an effective lead in secular society due to the loss of a sense of mission and direction. Without a clear sense of its own purpose, identity and destiny the church has been powerless to influence an increasingly secular society. A major cause of the church's loss of direction has been due to the lack of a clear concept of the meaning of history.

The twentieth century has seen more bloodshed (see my analysis 'A Century of Bloodshed' in *The Day Comes* [London: Collins, 1982], pp 157–159), human suffering, trauma and upheaval than any other century since the beginning of recorded history. This does not imply that there ever has been a century of peace, but the scale and numbers of those involved in the wars and disasters of this century make it unique. It is small wonder that throughout the world the closing years of the twentieth century are marked by massive disillusionment and fear of the future. Mankind is crying out for an understanding of history. This is of fundamental importance for grappling with the underlying issues concerning the meaning and purpose of life itself. The church will never be able to satisfy the deepest longings of mankind and give a lead to secular nations or point the way to creative policies promoting health, happiness and the well-being of mankind until Christians recover an understanding of history. An essential element in this is the recovery of confidence in the Bible as revealing a God who is the Lord of history and whose good purposes are being worked out in the unfolding story of humankind and of creation itself.

In much of the secular world, history has very little meaning or purpose as, for example, in existentialist philosophy where history is simply a meaningless succession of events. Hellenistic thought is no more helpful in providing a key to the understanding of history. The ancient Greeks thought of history in cyclical terms. John Marsh referred to the Greek cyclical view of history as depriving the whole of creation of any significance. He wrote:

> Just as the corn is sown, grows, and ripens each year, so will the events of history recur time after time. Moreover, if all that can happen is the constant repetition of an event-cycle, there is no possibility of meaning in the cycle itself. It achieves nothing in itself, neither can it contribute to anything outside itself. The events of history are devoid of significance. (John Marsh, *The Fullness of Time* [London: Nisbet, 1952], p 167.)

Similarly, Hinduism is based upon a cyclical view of creation with the endless repetition of life cycles. Such a view holds no prospect of meaning or purpose. It was to provide an escape from the endless repetition of life cycles that the Brahmin mendicants devised the concept of Nirvana through which those who achieve a certain level of holiness in their earthly existence may at last escape from the physical world and enter into a new form of existence.

The Bible, by contrast, not only sees God as being in control of history but also reveals a God who is purposive and who is active in working out those good purposes through the course of human history. Anthony Hoekema sees this revelation of God as the Lord of history as being central to the whole message of Scripture. He writes:

> Old Testament writers affirmed that God's Kingdom rules over all (Psalm 103:19), even over the kingdoms of the nations (2 Chronicles 20:6), and that he turns the heart of the king wherever he wishes (Proverbs 21:1). New Testament writers tell us that God accomplishes all things according to the counsel of his will (Ephesians 1:11), and that he has determined the times set for the nations of the earth and the exact

places where they should live (Acts 17:26). (A. A. Hoekema, *The Bible and the Future* [Exeter: Eerdmans, 1979] p 26.)

This understanding of God in control of the whole of history runs right through the Bible from Genesis to Revelation. God is not simply an abstract principle or impersonal transcendental force, he is personal, one who can be known by the people whom he created. He is known, not simply by what he says by those who are in a special relationship to him, but by his deeds, his actions in the world.

God was known to Israel, for example, as a God of salvation primarily through his action in saving Israel from slavery in Egypt. Throughout their history Israelites have looked back to that central act of God in their history as revealing the saving activity of God who heard their cries and responded by exercising his power over their oppressors. He thus revealed himself as Lord not simply of Israel, but of Egypt and of nations that did not acknowledge him. Isaiah makes an astounding statement about Cyrus, the Persian Emperor whom God used to release Israel from slavery in Babylon hundreds of years after the exodus from Egypt. The prophet records God saying of Cyrus, 'I summon you by name and bestow on you a title of honour, though you do not acknowledge me' (Is 45:4).

God's actions in human history had to be interpreted and this was one of the major roles of the prophets. Hence we find the word of God accompanying what the prophets knew as the 'deeds of the Lord'. Thus word and deed combined to bring the meaning of history to those who had eyes to see and ears to hear what God was communicating to the world.

In the New Testament we find that the deeds of the Lord are just as central to the message as they were in the Old Testament. On the Day of Pentecost Peter was able to declare with conviction what God had actually done, 'God has raised this Jesus to life, and we are all witnesses of the fact' (Acts 2:32). But just as the prophets had brought the word of the Lord to explain the significance of his actions, so Peter went on to declare, 'Therefore let all Israel be assured of this: God has made this Jesus, whom you crucified, both Lord and Christ' (v 36).

The sovereignty of God extending over all the nations is the constant message running all the way through the Bible. God looks for co-operation and expects it from those who are his faithful servants and who acknowledge his lordship over their lives, but that acknowledgement is not essential to the working out of the purposes of God. We see this in numerous accounts of the activity of God throughout Scripture. When Joseph was sold by his brothers into slavery in Egypt, that was certainly not God's desire, but God used it for the working out of his own purposes. When he revealed himself to his brothers Joseph said, 'It was not you who sent me here, but God' (Gen 45:8). And after the death of his father, Joseph reassured his brothers, 'Don't be afraid. Am I in the place of God? You intended to harm me, but God intended it for good to accomplish what is now being done, the saving of many lives' (Gen 50:19).

Thus God's control over history did not mean that this removed freedom of will from men and women, but rather that God was able to work out his purposes despite the non-co-operation, or even active opposition, of those who did not acknowledge him as Lord of all creation. What the brothers of Joseph had intended for evil, God used to work out his own good purposes.

In the same way God was able to use whole nations who did not acknowledge him as God. Isaiah referred to the Assyrians as the rod of God's anger whom he used to punish Jerusalem. 'I send him against a godless nation, I despatch him against a people who anger me . . . But this is not what he intends, this is not what he has in mind; his purpose is to destroy' (Is 10:5–7). Thus the prophet was able to say that once Assyria had served the purposes of God, that nation would be punished. 'I will punish the king of Assyria for the wilful pride of his heart' (v 12).

In the same way Cyrus the Persian was actually referred to as one who was 'anointed' by God (Is 45:1). This was certainly not a popular message and the prophet had to defend the word, declaring, 'This is what the Lord says—Do you question me about my children, or give me orders about the work of my hands? . . . I will raise up Cyrus in my righteousness; . . . he will rebuild my city and set my exiles free' (Is 45:11–13).

The Bible treats the history of all the nations, not just of Israel, as a working out of the purposes of God. He and he alone is the Lord of history. 'I am God, and there is no other; I am God, and there is none like me . . . My purpose will stand, and I will do all that I please . . . What I have said, that will I bring about; what I have planned that will I do' (Is 46:9–11).

The prophets were so convinced of God's absolute control over all the affairs of the nations; that even though many things happened which were abhorrent to God, such as the cruelty of the Assyrians in crushing Israel, he nevertheless remained in overall control and would use even the evil of wicked men and their cruelty finally to serve his own purposes. Thus Isaiah was able to declare with complete confidence that the day would come when God would crush the Assyrians and that this would be part of God's overall purpose for the nations. 'This is the plan determined for the whole world; this is the hand stretched out over all nations. For the Lord Almighty has purposed, and who can thwart him? His hand is stretched out, and who can turn it back?' (Is 14:25–27).

The Bible reveals a God who has plans for the whole world which cannot be thwarted. Once God has announced his purposes nothing can stand against him or prevent him from fulfilling his word. This understanding of God as the Lord of history is something which has very largely been lost by the western church. It has resulted in a powerlessness to declare the word of God with prophetic power and conviction in the second half of the twentieth century when all the nations have been shaken.

If we apply the biblical revelation of God as the Lord of history to events in the contemporary world, we should have to conclude that just as God brought about the fall of the mighty Assyrian army in the days of Isaiah so too he has been responsible for the fall of the mighty Communist empire led by the Soviet Union. In addition, the twentieth century has seen the fall of other seemingly unshakeable empires such as the Austro/Hungarian Empire, the cruel empire of the Third Reich, the mighty worldwide British Empire and all the colonial empires of the European nations. When God stretches out his hand and says that the time has come for a nation or a people, they can no longer stand.

The twentieth century has witnessed the disappearance of more empires than any other comparable period since the beginning of recorded history. This fact alone should make us stop and review the question of the meaning of history, a subject to which we shall return in Chapter 4. Such a study compels us to give credence to the message of the Bible that there is a purpose in history, but that purpose can only be understood in the context of a God who is Lord of all creation. When that message is properly understood it not only gives meaning to history, it gives meaning and purpose to the whole of life. It is the quest of that meaning and purpose in the context of contemporary world events which we shall pursue in this book.

2

Shaking the Foundations

The old, stable world of the Victorian era appeared unshakeable at the dawn of the twentieth century. The Boer War was still to be successfully concluded and although there had been a number of setbacks which had dented the pride of the British nation, their confidence in the outcome remained unshaken. Britannia ruled the waves, and her armies in any part of the world were invincible. Queen Victoria, nearing her Diamond Jubilee, ruled over the most extensive and most powerful empire the world had ever known. A 1906 government publication recorded the facts that the British Empire extended over one-fifth of the land surface of the globe, with a population in excess of 400 million.

The social structure of Britain was still essentially feudal. There was very little social mobility; people stayed in the social class into which they were born. The gap between the rich and the poor was almost unbridgeable, with sixty per cent of the employed in Britain working as servants to the rich. The latter, however, were comparatively few in number. The 1909 Liberal budget, hailed as the most radical in British history, introduced a new additional 'supertax' of sixpence in the pound to be levied on the people with incomes over £5,000 a year, of whom there were a mere 10,000. The standard rate of tax, however, remained unchanged at ninepence in the pound.

It was the 1914/18 war that began the great shaking of the nations. The European nations had parcelled out the world between them, reinforcing their trading capacity by annexation and colonisation. But in Europe itself the old social structure that had existed since mediaeval times remained largely unchanged, having survived the upheavals of the Napoleonic wars and even the Industrial Revolution. The latter, although it produced a new wealthy middle class (the owners of industry) and a new class of peasants (the urban landless poor), failed to share the advantages of the new source of wealth among the general population. In fact the nineteenth century saw a hardening of social divisions which carried over into the twentieth century not only a rigid social structure in which the poor were greatly disadvantaged, but also a fierce competition between the 'haves' and the 'have nots'. This was seen by Karl Marx and the Socialist leaders of the early twentieth century as a class war which could only be won through the destruction of capitalism and a fundamental change in the social order.

The old, stable world which had remained largely unchanged for centuries disappeared for ever into the mud and blood of Flanders. The 1914/18 conflict, although largely fought out on the soil of France, engulfed the whole world as the European nations called on the support of their colonies and as the USA was also drawn into the carnage. Britain lost more than three-quarters of a million men, and in addition a quarter of a million men from the British Empire also lost their lives. The overall casualties in four years of pointless slaughter were more than ten million killed, seventeen million wounded, of whom one-third were permanent invalids, having lost limbs, been blinded or gassed. Four million women were widowed and eight million children orphaned. The shortage of men affected a whole generation and left millions of single women to face the rest of their lives without a partner or children.

The political, economic and social fall-out from the First World War changed Europe for ever and was a watershed of fundamental change affecting the whole world. Mighty empires crumbled. The Austro/Hungarian Empire, the Russian Empire and the Ottoman Empire all fell as a direct result of World War One. The Chinese Empire also fell in this period. The Qing-Manchu dynasty which had lasted since 1644 finally ended in 1912.

The war in Europe furthered the demands among ordinary people for a greater share in prosperity and equality of status. Women had played a significant part in the war effort, which made their enfranchisement inevitable. Denmark (1915) was the first western nation to give the vote to women, followed by the Netherlands and Russia in 1917, Austria, Britain, Czechoslovakia, Poland and Sweden in 1918, Germany and Luxembourg in 1919 and the USA in 1920. The post-war period also saw the first Labour government in Britain (1924) but the world was already plunging into the worst international economic crisis ever known, due in part to the crippling reparations the Allies insisted on reaping from Germany where the mark in 1923 was virtually worthless, trading at twenty trillion marks to the pound sterling.

The inter-war years were a period of unemployment, social turmoil, poverty, misery and suffering for vast multitudes of people in the western industrialised nations. The foundations of the old stable world had begun to shake ever more violently, paving the way for the second half of the century which was to see the tearing away of the last remnants of the old world, the loss of all the old certainties and the challenge to every philosophical concept, ethical principle and moral and spiritual conviction on which the old world had rested for centuries.

The Second World War finally ended suddenly with the dropping of the atomic bombs which destroyed the cities of Hiroshima and Nagasaki. At that point the world entered the nuclear age and has lived in its shadow ever since; for the first time in history human beings had discovered and unleashed a power capable of destroying all life on the earth. That fear of global devastation has gripped the minds of men and women ever since, particularly during the dark days of the Cold War when the nations were divided into East and West, each sheltering behind their mighty nuclear arsenals. With the dissolution of the Soviet Union a new threat presented itself, as smaller and less stable nations began to acquire nuclear weapons. Reference has already been made (Chapter 1) to impoverished scientists and technicians in the CIS seeking to supplement their incomes by selling enriched plutonium to international criminals. Thus the components for making primitive nuclear bombs could easily fall into the hands of international terrorists who could hold whole nations to ransom.

Fear for the future and uncertainty has been growing in the world ever since the end of World War Two. The early post-war period of reconstruction which ran through the 1950s also saw the beginnings of the Cold War polarisation of Communism and Capitalism and the rise of a new socio-political force on the international scene—that of nationalism.

The Second World War resulted in a further redrawing of the map of the world with the division of Germany, the reshuffling of Eastern Europe within the orbit of the USSR and the dissolution of the Japanese Empire in the Far East. The second half of the twentieth century has also seen the dissolution of the remaining European empires. An era that began with the colonial conquests of the fifteenth and sixteenth centuries came to an end in the wave of tribalism and nationalism that has been sweeping the world throughout the second half of the century, resulting in the clamour for independence from even the smallest identifying people group.

Powerful European nations were unable to hold on to their colonies as the spread of modern weapons throughout the world gave colonial rebels the ability to fight the empires. The British, the French, the Dutch, the Belgian, the Spanish and the Portuguese have all surrendered their empires with varying degrees of willingness. The French fought bitterly for Indo-China which led directly to the American/Vietnam debacle, as the USA refused to contemplate a Communist takeover of the region. The Dutch were thrown out of Indonesia and the Portuguese resisted in Mozambique and Angola. Africa gradually threw off the yoke of European imperialism, but the colonial legacy undoubtedly contributed to the tribal conflicts and civil wars that have claimed the lives of millions in Zaire, Angola, Chad, Nigeria, Mozambique, Zimbabwe, Uganda, Algeria, Ethiopia, Sudan, Rwanda, Burundi and South Africa.

The lasting consequences of the European colonial era are that it has brought western ideas, values and technology into every part of the world, with all its advantages as well as its miseries. The resultant disturbance of whole population groups, the mixing of tribes, the breaking down of tradition, the spread of urbanisation, the redrawing of national boundaries and the growth of new nations with new identities has brought about an unprecedented period of worldwide change. This has been a direct cause of the tragic conflicts we have seen in Yugoslavia, the States of the former USSR, the tribal conflicts in many parts of the African continent, such as the Nigerian civil war, the genocide in Burundi and conflicts in Sudan and Ethiopia, as well as the problems in the Indian sub-continent and Asia. The twentieth century has witnessed an unprecedented shaking of the political, social and cultural foundations in every part of the world. This mixing of races and cultures may in the long term produce greater harmony and stability, but in the short term its effects have been destabilising.

The twentieth century has seen spectacular developments in technology which have carried it from the world of the horse and cart to interplanetary exploration. Revolutionary developments in communications and travel have transformed the world into a global village, which has had a further destabilising effect, not only through mass migration and the mixing of races, cultures and religions, but also through the technological advances in themselves. These have brought great advantages in improving the quality of life and transforming the life-style of millions, especially in the rich nations. But automation, computers and other technological advances have combined with increased competition and the drive to reduce costs and maximise profits in a capitalist economy. These have reduced the need for labour, resulting in high levels of unemployment in the rich industrialised nations. This has combined with a number of other factors to produce a mood of disenchantment with science and technology that began to sweep across the industrialised world in the 1980s.

Public awareness of the threat to the environment by industrialisation and urbanisation, by the destruction of rain forests and the ozone layer, the pollution of the atmosphere as well as the land and the sea, are all problems of the modern world. They have combined with the recession and high levels of unemployment, to produce a wave of resentment against further modernisation and calls for simpler lifestyles. The invention of weapons of mass destruction, the horrific possibilities of biological warfare or nuclear destruction have strengthened the anti-technology lobby. The ethics of genetic experiments and 'spare-parts surgery' have been increasingly questioned, while science is blamed for many of the ills assailing the modern world, such as animal diseases like BSE and the resultant genetic disorders following the nuclear power disaster at Chernobyl.

The twentieth century, which began with such high hopes of achieving a brave new world, has in reality been the century of shattered dreams. As the foundations of the old order were shaken and the old certainties disappeared, a new order began to be birthed based on technology, scientific advancement, rationalism, existentialism and moral relativity. None of these developments has brought satisfaction, rather they have increased the sense of insecurity and fear for the future. Millions of people feel powerless as the evidence mounts that the world is being driven by forces beyond the power of humanity to control. Technological advances which solve one set of problems serve to create other, even more intractable problems.

It is not only the poor who feel powerless—the rich and the powerful feel equally helpless. In Britain the middle and upper classes are suffering most from the loss of status and privileges which they once took for granted. The British working classes had not had any social status until the post-World-War-Two economic boom gave them a purchasing power they had never before known.

At the same time the rise of the pop culture gave a new status to youth. It shifted the balance of popular prestige from age to youth for the first time in the history of Britain. The welfare state, the National Health Service, pensions and allowances all sought to remove the age-old curse of poverty. But with the onslaught of recession in the late eighties and early nineties the old insecurities and fears assailed the working classes again and threatened a return to the class warfare that has continually dogged British society and undermined economic prosperity. The greed of the rich and the intransigence of organised labour combined to produce the economic and social disasters that have littered the pages of British social history since the early days of the Industrial Revolution.

The 1990s, however, have seen a new social phenomenon, the relative deprivation of the ruling classes. A combination of the advances in technology and the economic recession of the nineties hit all classes of society. In some ways the greatest impact was felt among the middle and upper middle classes who previously had found ways of sheltering from the storm in times of economic stringency. White-collar workers, professionals and managerial groups had enjoyed lifetime job security. All this suddenly disappeared. Computers could do the work of hundreds of people; managers were expendable; even professionals found their lifetime jobs replaced by short-term contracts. Insecurity, once confined to wage workers, now began to encompass the nation at all levels. The great Stock Market crash of 1987 had generated fresh levels of fear and uncertainty which continued into the 1990s as the recession deepened. The vagaries of the market and lower interest rates drastically reduced the income of those who relied upon investment.

The economic problems of the 1990s have been worldwide. In Britain multitudes of individuals and families have been struggling with insurmountable debts. Bankruptcies, debt foreclosure and repossession of houses have become commonplace in the context of high levels of unemployment. Additionally, the introduction of contract employment, which has become increasingly com-

monplace in the nineties, has added to the general level of
uncertainty and instability in society. Many firms have
adopted the practice of dismissing their long-term staff
and re-engaging them, or taking on others, on a short-term
contractual basis. This practice is becoming increasingly
common, not only at a blue collar level, but among white
collar workers and professionals and is extended even to
the higher grades of management. Thus job security is
rapidly becoming a thing of the past and continuance of
employment is dependent upon performance.

This creates difficulties with young couples wishing to
marry, take on a mortgage and have children. Many young
couples are fearful of the future and shy away from long-
term relationship commitments, preferring simply to live
together and take life a day at a time. Gone are the days
when young people could look forward to a lifetime
working in a single firm, or a lifetime of service in a
particular profession with the security of knowing that
they would always have employment and thus be able to
plan their lives, financial commitment and family responsibilities. Even the clergy today are no longer being
offered a 'living', with security of tenure for as long as
they feel called to that particular church or parish, but they
are being offered limited contracts with any renewal being
dependent upon performance.

All these changes in family life, and the contractual
basis of employment, together with the fear generated in
society through rising crime rates and increasing levels of
violence with media reports on vicious crimes perpetrated
against the elderly and weakest and most vulnerable in
society, raise the level of stress being experienced by
every individual today. This high level of stress, which
is running right through society at all levels, is a significant factor affecting the physical and mental health of
millions of people today. In America millions of people

regularly consult psychiatrists and in Britain the counselling services, which are comparatively new institutions, are grossly overloaded in most parts of the country. Stress levels are particularly high in the south-east of England where millions commute into London and the pressures of performance-related employment are very high.

The church has not been immune from these high levels of stress in society. All churches are affected. Pastors, ministers and priests—all who have any pastoral responsibility—are feeling the impact of the strains in the nation. It is not only those who are in full-time ministry who are affected but also many lay leaders who share in pastoral responsibilities. They too bear the strain of the high levels of stress in the lives of those to whom they have pastoral responsibilities. The stresses and strains of the pastoral ministry have been responsible for a great deal of problems in the lives of those in ministry, such as burn-out, nervous breakdown, marital strain and breakdown, as well as men leaving the pastoral ministry or taking early retirement.

The church, of course, is not the only institution to be suffering from the high levels of stress in society. Education has been particularly affected over the past ten years or so, with many teachers leaving the profession as they are unable to cope with the high levels of stress in the classroom, plus the constant changes within the educational system. In most schools today, with the majority of children coming from broken homes and suffering various degrees of trauma, teachers are forced into pastoral roles for which they are not qualified, which adds to the stress they experience.

These high levels of stress in society are having a significant effect upon the mission of the church. The question needs to be faced: Is this a great distraction, turning the church aside from its primary task of evangelism and declaring the message of the kingdom at what is undoubtedly a highly significant period in world history? Ministers are weary and overloaded with problems, often struggling to maintain churches in difficult areas with inadequate resources. They themselves often face personal problems in marriage and family relationships and when they are constantly called upon to bear the burdens of others and to give counsel to those caught up in seemingly impossible situations, the stress is often unbearable.

It is possible to see the stress in society not simply in terms of a distraction from the mission of the church, but as an opportunity for service. Nineteenth-century Britain was not a period of social tranquillity! Indeed, at the beginning of that century there were still strong fears that Britain might experience a social upheaval similar to the horrors of the French Revolution and levels of stress throughout the nation were high, particularly in relationships between the rich and the poor.

Nineteenth-century evangelicals in Britain saw this as a challenge and an opportunity to serve the nation. They responded by setting up schools, hospitals, hostels, orphanages and many other institutions to meet the needs of the community. Additionally, they entered fully into the political as well as social spheres of life, campaigning relentlessly to change social conditions. They were largely responsible for many far-reaching changes in the law, such as the abolition of slavery, the prohibition of children working in mines and factories for long hours and the introduction of compulsory education for all children.

It is possible for the church at the end of the twentieth century to respond to the social conditions of today by making provision to meet the needs of society. Those needs can be met by providing additional resources for counselling and making them available, not only to regular churchgoers, but also to others in the community.

This is a very positive form of needs-based evangelism which has a proven track record.

The church can also respond prophetically to current social conditions by explaining the reasons why the nations are being shaken to their foundations and why the British, in particular, are experiencing such high levels of stress. We shall be returning in some detail to the shaking of the nations and the biblical witness concerning these things. At this point we are noting the British situation wherein the second half of the twentieth century has seen a collective loss of national confidence.

The crumbling of the British Empire and the gradual loosening of ties within the British Commonwealth of nations has resulted in a massive loss of national status. The second half of the twentieth century has seen Britain's role on the international scene shrink from a major world political and economic power to one of the also-rans. The British armed forces have been drastically reduced in all three services. Britain no longer rules the waves or has the power to influence the world. National pride has been humbled as the foundations of Britain's international power base have been eroded.

This loss of national prestige has affected the privileged classes more than the poor and has been one of the major causes of the inept and uncertain political leadership exercised by the Conservative government in the late 1980s and in the 1990s. The shaking of the foundations has created a basic uncertainty in leadership. The things the rich trusted in and took for granted are no longer secure. Wealth no longer lies in the ownership of land; inherited titles are no longer the 'open sesame' to success in the world. Many of the aristocracy have become impoverished, others have lost their estates and many of the upper middle classes have lost their country houses, their London flats and their second or third cars. By the mid-

1990s the days of the House of Lords appear to be numbered and the monarchy itself, heart of the Establishment, seems bent on self-destruction as it reels from one self-induced scandal to the next.

The foundations of the British nation which have held firm through centuries of change, and have successfully resisted the impact of two world wars, are now beginning to crumble. The marital problems within the Royal Family, including the Prince of Wales' public confession of adultery, and the publicity given to a succession of their personal problems, has shaken the nation's confidence in their First Family. For hundreds of years the monarchy has been the central institution in the British Establishment and a symbol of stability. It has provided the nation with a sheet anchor of constancy and durability, enabling it to weather the storms of political and social change.

Traditionally the British monarchy has played an important role in giving unity and stability to the nation, not only as a symbol of enduring values in the social structure of the nation, but also in its moral and spiritual principles. The Coronation Oath, in which the monarch pledges to uphold the Protestant faith, gives assent to the biblical foundations of the moral precepts undergirding the nation both in its corporate and personal relationships.

In a televised interview in May 1994 Prince Charles made it clear that he no longer accepts a biblically based faith. He stated that he would see himself as 'upholding faith, rather than *the* faith'. He justified this by referring to the presence of people of different religions in Britain and the Commonwealth. But if such a fundamental change were to be made to the Coronation Oath it would be a repudiation of the Judeo/Christian heritage which has undergirded the nation for centuries.

Prince Charles' views have been known for a long time, especially among those with leadership responsibilities in the nation. They were also aware of his marital problems and of the difficulties and tensions within the Royal Family long before these became public knowledge. These difficulties, together with the succession of scandals involving people of prominence in the political and commercial life of the nation, have all had an unsettling effect. They have contributed to weak vacillating leadership, which has been exacerbated by the international economic problems and the increasing complexities of international relationships for which there seem to be no rational answers.

All these factors have combined to shake the foundations of the nation, not only in its corporate life, but also in the personal affairs of every individual citizen. No one can remain unshaken when the nation itself is going through a period of violent and revolutionary change. When we are in the midst of a storm it is difficult to reflect calmly upon the situation and make far-reaching decisions. It is not easy even to see the direction the storm is taking or to assess where the next thunderbolt will strike. All this has a destabilising effect upon every aspect of the life of a nation and its citizens.

It is in such times that the beliefs of a nation and of each individual are severely tested. Where there is no firmly anchored faith there is no stability—we are blown about by every change in the direction of the wind. Jesus contrasted the fate of the house built upon sand, which was unable to withstand the impact of the storm and the house which was built upon a rock, whose foundations held firmly against the violence of the winds of change.

A biblically based faith not only gives us a fixed reference point and provides us with a firm set of values with which to judge the changes which are occurring, but it also provides us with a hope for the future. That hope is linked with our understanding of the purpose of life and indeed with our understanding of the whole purpose underlying creation. This has been revealed by God to his servants the prophets and through the life, death and resurrection of Jesus. God does not wish us to be in ignorance of his purposes. Neither does he wish us to be driven by fear of the unknown or to feel powerless, which is the experience of millions of people in the world today. That sense of powerlessness, of being driven by forces outside our control, is dispelled by a firm faith in God.

Jesus called his disciples 'friends'. He said, 'I no longer call you servants, because a servant does not know his master's business. Instead, I have called you friends, for everything I have learned from my Father I have made known to you' (Jn 15:15). Through faith in Jesus we have the incredible privilege of being taken into God's confidence! The fog of confusion which hangs as a heavy cloud over the nations is dispersed, the light dawns and we are able to understand what is happening in the world around us. We are living in a period of incredible change, one of the most exciting periods of history since the creation. It is the purpose of this book to try to unravel the sequence of events in the contemporary world scene and to note their significance. In the next two chapters we shall make first a sociological approach, and then a biblical approach.

3

The Processes of Change

In attempting to identify the forces of change which are sweeping through the contemporary world, it is helpful first to look at the structure of society and the function of its constituent parts. In so doing we will use the British situation as a model, although in sociological terms our analysis could apply to most nations in the western world. As a general rule it is worth noting that there are basic similarities between all the industrialised nations, particularly those coming within the orbit of what may be loosely described as western culture. Culture is a major determinant of the function of social institutions. To express that more simply, the cultural traditions of a society have a major influence upon human behaviour in all aspects of our corporate and personal relationships. Non-industrial societies are largely governed by tribal custom and they function in a very different way from industrial societies.

In British society, typical of western industrialised societies, for the purpose of analysis the sociologist looks at society in terms of social institutions. There are hundreds of social institutions; for example, a local tennis club, or cricket club, or working men's institution, a school, a university, a hospital, a factory—each of these is a social institution. It is an identifiable unit in society within which human beings function, have particular relationships to each other and carry out different roles, performing different tasks and achieving identifiable ends or goals.

There are, however, five major social institutions recognised by sociologists within which we can analyse the structure and function of any complex industrialised society. They are:

(1) The family
(2) The economy
(3) Law (government and law enforcement)
(4) Education
(5) Religion

These five constitute the basic structure of the social system and we shall use each of them as a heading for our analysis of the processes of change which have been at work in twentieth-century Britain.

(1) The family

It is not easy to define a family. We use the term in so many different ways. It can mean simply a mother and father and children, either procreated or adopted. But if one of the parents dies or is divorced it is still a family. We then refer to it as a single-parent family. But when the children grow up and move away we speak of the family having left home. Or when we become grandparents we speak about the family visiting us. Or if there are lots of children and grandchildren we speak of the family coming together for Christmas. But when there is a wedding in the family and aunts and uncles and in-laws, and others related by marriage, or cousins and second cousins are all invited, we speak about 'the whole family' coming together.

However we define the family, whether as a simple

nuclear unit or the larger all-embracing extended family, its function within society is of major significance. The family regulates the relationships within the generations. It helps to define our place in society. It gives us the security and identity of kinship. The family regulates the ownership of property and inheritance, it defines our role within the family unit and regulates the early socialisation of children, teaches social values and standards of behaviour, including sexual behaviour.

(2) The economy

The economy as a major social institution embraces the whole area of work, whether it is corporate employment or self-employment. It is concerned with the production of goods, their distribution and sale. It is concerned with exchange and commerce, with interest rates, banking, finance, investment, credit and debt.

The economy in a modern urban industrial society is incredibly complex and embraces the whole subject of economic activity, from individual consumer demand to the complexities of the national budget and international trade.

(3) Law

Law includes the whole system by which a society is governed, that is, the way in which its laws are formulated and enforced. Basically it is concerned with the exercise of power within the society, its allocation and restraint. Our system of law largely determines the social order, its construction and maintenance. Laws are formulated by the legislature which, in a democracy, is an elected assembly of representatives. But once the law has been enacted it has to be enforced and maintained through law enforcement officers and the judicial service, through magistrates courts and higher courts. For offenders there are also the prison and probation services. Thus law and government play an important part in maintaining the traditions of acceptable behaviour within a society and contribute towards its stability.

(4) Education

Education includes every aspect of learning. The process of socialisation is that by which the culture of a society is passed on from one generation to the next. It commences at birth when the baby begins to discover its environment and to learn to function within a social context. The parents teach the child right or wrong by expressing pleasure or displeasure, approval or disapproval. It is largely within the family and peer group that we learn the mores of the community and we adopt acceptable standards of behaviour.

Education also includes the formal institutions of school, college, university and professional bodies. In its broadest sense education never ceases—we are always learning until the day we die. Thus education includes the sum total of our acquired knowledge, the accumulated wisdom and culture of the whole society which is passed on from generation to generation. It also includes the means of transmission and acquisition of that knowledge.

(5) Religion

Religion is a sphere of human activity that is extremely difficult to define. Through religion we are dealing with the transcendental, that which is outside the material, space/time world in which we all exist. Religion deals with concepts that are often indefinable, such as faith and personal conviction, and which are often difficult to define in terms of purely rational propositions. Through religion we ascribe 'worthship' to that which is outside ourselves whom we define as God and whose authority we acknowledge over our lives.

Religion also has to do with the fundamental values which we acknowledge in our lives. These also define our moral behaviour. They are the ethical standards by which we judge right and wrong and which give content to our personal and corporate judgement of quality, worth or behaviour.

Summary

The table opposite provides a summary of the five major social institutions and their function within the total social system.

The dynamics of social change

Change is a characteristic of all human societies, even those that appear to be static, such as those based on a system of caste. All living organisms experience change and thus society, which is the aggregate of individuals within it, has similar dynamics to those of the human body, even though the change may be extremely slow and only noticeable over a very long period of time.

Within the total social system each of the five major social institutions undergoes change. For example, the family in Britain has changed fundamentally during the twentieth century. In 1900 the basic characteristic was the extended family. Due to the lack of mobility, both geographical and social, several generations of the family

Major social institutions

Institution	Factors Regulated
The family	kinship • property • inheritance • relationships between the generations • sexual behaviour • familial roles
The economy	work • production • distribution • exchange • commerce • finance • banking • investment
Government and law	allocation and restraint of power • social order • legislation and law enforcement • police • courts • prison service
Education	socialisation • formal learning systems • schools • professional institutions • universities
Religion	belief systems • worship • values • moral behaviour

lived in close proximity, usually within a mile or so. Thus the family included grandparents, parents and children, as well as aunts, uncles and cousins, all living within a single neighbourhood and able to give support to one another and function together as an identifiable social unit.

By the middle of the century the basic characteristics had changed to that of the nuclear family; that is, mother and father and their offspring living together in a single dwelling, usually in isolation from the rest of their kin. By the beginning of the 1990s eighteen per cent of all families were headed by a single parent, and single-parent families were found to be the fastest growing social group in Britain. Thus in the course of one century the family underwent fundamental structural changes. These changes affected relationships within the family, sexual behaviour and, even more importantly, the socialisation of children, teaching them basic morality, standards of behaviour within society, relationships with others and social attitudes.

The economy has also undergone basic changes during the twentieth century, culminating in the technological revolution currently being experienced. There have been basic changes in the law and law enforcement. There have been fundamental changes in religion in Britain, not only through the decline in church attendance, but also due to immigration, which has resulted in Britain becoming a multi-faith society. There have also been fundamental changes in both the philosophy and practice of education in our schools and universities. The method of teaching pupils is radically different in the classrooms of today, with their computers, language laboratories and scientific equipment, from the classrooms of the Dame schools or elementary schools of the Victorian era.

We may therefore assert with confidence that each of the major social institutions has been experiencing fundamental changes which have occurred during the twentieth century. It is an established sociological precept that each of the major social institutions has a direct effect upon the others. Therefore, whenever change is experienced within one social institution, all the others are affected.

A good example of this principle, illustrating the dynamics of social change, is the Industrial Revolution. The invention of the steam engine and the introduction of mechanical means of production not only produced basic changes in the economy in terms of the means of production, distribution and exchange, thus forming the basis of industrialisation; but it also affected all the other major social institutions, changing for ever the lives of the entire population.

The development of industry demanded labour, which drew people from the countryside into the rapidly growing towns and changed the family from rural peasants to an urban population with consequent basic changes in life-style for each member of the family. An urban population needed a different form of social order. New laws had to be passed and a system of law enforcement, police and magistrates courts had to be established to meet the new situation. An urban population brought together people from different areas of the country and even from over-seas, with their different cultures, religious beliefs and practices. An urban industrial population also needed education which had to be formalised, although it was not until 1870 that education became compulsory for every child in the land.

All these changes came about through the Industrial Revolution. What began as a basic change within the economy triggered off a process of change within each of the other social institutions.

The changes which have swept across the world during the second half of the twentieth century have made it a unique period of history. The rate of change has acceler-ated rapidly. This has been due to the fact that each of the major social institutions has been experiencing change generated within itself and has thereby been affecting each of the others. Thus changes have come from both directions, from within the institution and from each of the others. Changes in the economy producing new technol-ogy such as videos and computers have required new legislation to control their use and to counter abuse. Changes within the family have affected the economy, with more elderly people drawing pensions and single parents to be supported. Conversely, new technology and recession in the economy have affected the family through unemployment or the relocation of jobs. We could continue looking at the way religion has changed and education has changed and their effects upon the family or upon law or conversely. Such illustrations could be multiplied many times over.

The point we are making is that the second half of the twentieth century has seen a unique situation in which each of the major social institutions has been generating fundamental changes within itself which has affected each of the other institutions. At the same time those changes have generated further changes with a seesaw effect running right through the whole social system. As each change has occurred so it has generated further changes, causing the whole process of change to accelerate. As the rate of change has increased at an ever-increasing rate, so the whole process has speeded up like an aeroplane beginning to spin out of control. As the angle of descent increases so the rate of descent increases. And as the speed increases so too does the violence of the spin, thus shaking the structure of the aircraft beyond its capacity, with inevitable results.

Something like that has been happening in Britain throughout the second half of the twentieth century. Changes in one part of the social system have triggered changes in others, with a build-up effect resulting in a rapid acceleration of the rate of change running right the way through every part of the social structure and affecting the life of the nation both in corporate affairs and in individual lives. The build-up effect of changes within each major social institution has accelerated change within the whole, with the resultant destabilising of the life of the nation.

This destabilisation has occurred through a major disturbance of the social value system which forms the foundations upon which the whole life of the nation is built. The value system is built by the beliefs, the ethical principles—moral precepts which are accumulated by the nation over the course of centuries. They are usually difficult to define, being rooted in spiritual concepts rather than material things. They nevertheless have a very important function in the life of the nation and once disturbed they are difficult to replace. When the foundations of a building crumble it is not long before the whole building collapses.

The October 1987 hurricane-force wind, which hit south-east England, provided a dramatic parable of what was happening in the national life. In the two or three hours of winds in excess of a hundred miles an hour racing across the south coast towards London and out into the north sea, sixteen million trees were reported to have been destroyed. The hurricane followed four years of drought during which there had been insufficient moisture to feed the roots. The ground around the roots had dried out and cracked, further loosening the trees' grip upon the earth, leaving them vulnerable when the great storm struck.

For many years the faith of the nation has been in decline with the decrease in church attendance, the increase in secularism and the impact of other religions. The foundational beliefs of the nation have not been fed and watered. As the winds of change have begun blowing ever more strongly across the nation, the fate of the sixteen million trees may be taken as a symbol of the disaster that lies ahead unless there is a dramatic change and a slowing down of the rate of change, a re-emphasis upon fundamental social values and a rebuilding of secure foundations to undergird the life of the nation.

Value system

In order to give some further clarification of the way the foundational value system of the nation has been disturbed we have to go back to the middle of the twentieth century. The immediate aftermath of the Second World War was not only a period of physical reconstruction in Europe following the ravages of war and intensive aerial bombing, it was also a period of rethinking social values and policies.

In Britain this resulted in a landslide victory for the Labour Party and the introduction of radical new policies such as the welfare state, free medical care, national insurance and state ownership of basic industries. It was a period of great optimism and openness to new ideas. There was a real desire to establish permanent peace in the world and to discard the old ideals which had plunged the world into two devastating wars in the first half of the century. The formation of the United Nations, plus the increasing facilities for travel and communication between the nations, gave hope to the ideal of a brave new world. A major cloud on the international horizon, however, was the shadow of the atomic bomb and the fear of a nuclear holocaust. The post-war scramble among the powerful nations to arm themselves with the latest weapons fuelled the fires of fear and gave impetus to the anti-nuclear campaigners.

The Peace Movement was part of a broader movement of social idealism seeking to leave behind the old values of inequality and injustice which had led to poverty and the exploitation of the masses. Foremost in the thinking of the social idealists was the rejection of social manipulation through indoctrination of political or social ideals. Prime targets were fascism and racism. These twin philosophies had led to the evil of Nazism built on the Aryan myth of racial superiority which had been fed to a whole generation of German youth and had directly led to the central European holocaust, in which six million Jews had died in concentration camps and millions of civilians and service personnel had lost their lives in the war.

The rejection of indoctrination, propaganda and manipulation gave rise to the positive desire for 'value freedom'; the social conditions in which each individual could decide for themselves the values they would uphold. It was in response to this search for value freedom that the social sciences rose to the height of their popularity in the 1960s and 1970s. Sociology was, for a time, the most popular subject for study among degree students. Most sociology courses were heavily Marxist in content. The London School of Economics led the way in establishing the political correctness of the day and it was often said that the LSE was more Marxist than Moscow, and its students would take to the streets to support any radical demonstration or join the picket lines of protestors for any subversive cause likely to embarrass those in authority.

The target of the protestors was not simply the Establishment or the bourgeoisie—traditional enemies of the proletariat—but any in positions of authority or power, even those attempting to carry out Socialist policies. The 1960s were a period of revolutionary social change generated by the 'social Darwinism', or Utopianism, that flowed from the new concepts being taught in sociology and the allied social sciences.

This social idealism was aided and abetted by the post-war boom in the economy which produced an unprecedented demand for labour. This in turn drew waves of immigrants into Britain from the Commonwealth, but more importantly it gave wealth to new social groups, especially the young. Young people were able to leave school and command high wages for the first time ever.

The significance of this for the economy soon became apparent but the long-term social significance was not immediately seen. In the 1950s and 1960s young people began earning high wages. They thus became a consumer group with high spending power, ripe for exploitation in a free market economy. These young people were less discriminating in their purchasing patterns than their parents. They had money in their pockets and they had fewer responsibilities than older people, being free from mortgages and family obligations. The market rapidly moved to produce the kind of goods that would appeal to young people—clothes, hi-fis and leisure goods.

The social effects of the rise of this new consumer group were revolutionary. Traditionally Britain had been a society in which age was honoured. Suddenly the trend was towards youth. The pop culture of the 1960s, symbolised by the music of the Beatles, the Rolling Stones and numerous other groups, signalled the end of traditional values and the rise of the new anti-authority libertarianism.

Politicians caught the new mood of the public looking for freedom, self-expression and a break with tradition. The 1960s saw laws going onto the Statute Book in Westminster that represented a radical break with the past and introduced a new era of public and personal morality. In the public domain there was important legislation outlawing racial and sexual discrimination, as well as the removal of censorship, which led to the promotion of pornography in art, literature, film and theatre. In the sphere of personal morality there was legislation legalising abortion, easier divorce and a range of other measures giving greater freedom to the individual and the liberty to decide upon issues of morality.

Simultaneously, with the continued decline in churchgoing, Sunday schools and biblical teaching in schools, there was no longer a clear set of moral principles and ethical values as a point of reference for those seeking guidance in moral decision making for either personal behaviour or in the public domain. The 1960s and 1970s saw Britain entering a period of moral anarchy in which there were no ultimate values. Without a yardstick in a period of rapid and radical social change, society was dangerously adrift.

In order to give further understanding of the processes of change at work in Britain at the end of the twentieth century, it may be helpful to look briefly at the three-generational cycle of social change. This is an hypothesis developed by sociologists to account for the generational differences which appear to occur in many societies. It involves a degree of caricaturing the different generations but this does serve to highlight some important social characteristics which reveal areas of tension and stress in the population where there are strongly held differences in social attitudes.

The three generations are as follows:

(1) Those born before 1945 who experienced the dark and difficult days of depression and the dangerous days of World War Two.
(2) Those born between 1945 and 1969 who grew up in the booming post-war era, many of whom reached adolescence and early maturity in the promiscuous 1960s.
(3) Those born since 1970 who have experienced the years of disillusionment, when the hopes of a better world and a brighter future were fading into the harsh realities of the 1980s, the world of famine, terrorism, AIDS and economic recession.

We may label these three generations in terms of their social attitudes; the generations of 'The Hopers', 'The Boomers' and 'The Busters'.

The Hopers, born into a world of harsh reality, knew what it was to struggle for existence yet hoped for a better world. They were prepared to go to war and pay the ultimate price in the struggle against human evil and economic depression. They endured the hardship of slump, unemployment and war, but always with the hope that the struggle was worthwhile and there would be better times ahead.

This was a generation willing to endure hardship for the sake of future generations, prepared to make self-sacrifice for the benefit of others. It was a generation where the dominant social value was one of delayed rewards, which produced attitudes of unselfishness, being prepared to share and to give rather than simply to get and to gain. It was a generation longing to give their children all the advantages they had been denied which, in the event, was to prove less than healthy for the next generation.

The Boomers were born in the post-war baby boom era of the late 1940s, 1950s and early 1960s. This was the time when the nations were still basking in the glow of victory or licking the wounds of defeat, but all were rebuilding from the ravages of war. It was an age of reconstruction and growth. Hopes were at their highest, the brave new world was emerging, consumer demand was booming and the economy was expanding rapidly. The shops were full again, money was plentiful, and parents delighted to indulge their children. The age of consumerism had dawned. The destructive values of acquisitiveness and naked materialism were birthed.

The pop culture, the introduction of television, the powerful advertising media, the generation of young people with high spending power and low social responsibilities, all combined to produce a social revolution.

A new breed of teachers, with a new educational philosophy, fuelled the social revolution. Children were encouraged to think for themselves rather than to learn by rote, to challenge authority rather than to obey it, and to question tradition rather than simply accept it. The social values, including morals and religion of past generations were spurned. This was a new day and the public mood was intent upon establishing new morality and new social values. It was a generation of idealism, despising most of what had gone before as part of an out-moded society.

The Boomers initiated the dawn of an age of new morality, of ethical relativity in which each situation was to be judged on its own merits, with no ultimate standard. But it did not produce the desired social Utopia! The brave new world emerged tarnished and flawed as crime rates soared, the gap between rich and poor widened, and racism, prejudice and the exploitation of the powerless still existed. The world was still at war in numerous localised conflicts. The threat of a nuclear holocaust hovered over the nations. Idealism began to fade into disillusionment.

The Busters, born after 1970, are the physical firstfruits of the Boomers. They have none of the values which had been passed on to their parents by the Hopers. The values transmitted to them were those of *laissez-faire*—do what you like, when you like, how you like. Born into a world idealising freedom and opportunism, they lacked the idealism of their parents. They grew up into a world of unrealised dreams, when the reality of the present was rapidly souring the hopes of the past. The social revolution which was to bring freedom from poverty, freedom from fear, freedom from violence and establish love and peace in the world had simply not succeeded.

The Busters were children of broken dreams. They reached adolescence and grew to maturity in the 1980s, when the world was still divided between east and west, but the disillusionment with radical Marxist principles was already threatening to break up the great Communist empires which had been founded upon the hopes of the masses. These hopes of freedom from exploitation by the ruling classes had disappeared in the blood of the victims of violent purges by the Communist dictators. In the same way the hopes of the people for prosperity had disappeared in the harsh realities of poverty and broken promises.

The Busters were born into a world where the hopes of peace were fading as war followed war in a never-ending cycle of violence, as weapons became more destructive and local conflicts threatened to engulf the entire globe. Vietnam, Afghanistan, Lebanon, the Falklands, Iraq/Iran, the Gulf War, Yugoslavia, Rwanda, plus the continuing escalation of international terrorism, were all vividly portrayed on TV newscasts.

The eighties was the decade of disillusionment, the end of the road of idealism. It was the decade of drugs, despair, unemployment, poverty and AIDS—the bitter fruit of the dreams of the past. The Busters can see the failures of the past but they have no answers to dilemmas of the present, so they lack hope for the future. The gap between rich and poor appears unbridgeable. The revelations of greed, corruption and untrustworthiness among those holding high office and positions of responsibility in society have given rise to a generation having no trust in its leaders. Even political revolution provides no lasting answers to the problems of humanity. The Busters have witnessed the demise of Communism and the end of political idealism. Theirs is a world of mass famine, of mass deaths through plague and disease. With no cure in sight for AIDS the only advice their free thinking parents can give them is to wear a condom!

The Busters are a generation of individuals—yuppies at

one end, yobs at the other, each with an essentially individualistic and socially destructive philosophy of life. Many have basic anti-social attitudes with no real desire to participate in society, let alone to improve it.

The contrast between the generations is strong and may be summarised by their attitude to life. For the Hopers it was a philosophy of delayed rewards, 'pay now and enjoy the fruit later'; for the Boomers it was 'have now, pay later'; for the Busters it is 'take now, for there may not be a future'.

The Busters have a socially destructive attitude. They see no reason to care for property which they can never own; so they enjoy vandalism, use spray cans to spread graffiti, steal cars, go joy-riding, sniff solvents, take crack and have casual sex, ignoring the dangers because life has little or no meaning or purpose for them.

The major question facing the twenty-first century is: Will the three-generational cycle be repeated? The Busters, who care for neither God nor man, do not yet hold major political or economic power. Most of them have no wish to do so. Will they so completely destroy their world that their children will have to start all over again and struggle through an age of deprivation, hardship and suffering? The greatest problem facing the Buster generation is that they do not have the inherited social stability of previous generations. Many do not even have the advantage of stable family and home life, with the love and belongingness which come from a mother, father and siblings.

The Busters are not the first generation to be born into a world of violence, but they are the first generation to be born into the world of video, of uncensored film and literature, of explicit sex, rape and murder brought into the sitting-room. It is a world where children are no longer protected from the realities of the adult world, are often subjected to abuse, witness domestic violence and lack the protection of a secure home and family environment. It is a world from which the basic principles of right and wrong and spiritual values have been eroded as the biblically based foundations of the nation have been shaken.

4

The Meaning of History

In Chapter 1 we spoke of the God of history and we expressed the view that the biblical understanding of history is that of the unfolding revelation of the purposes of God. In this chapter we want to carry those thoughts further and pose the question, 'What is the goal towards which history is moving?'

The biblical revelation of the purposes of God may be summarised under five headings—

(1) God's intention to bring humanity into a right relationship with himself through Christ
(2) Christ is the centre-point of history
(3) The new age has already dawned, the kingdom of God is here
(4) The ultimate goal is a new heaven and a new earth
(5) The strategy of God is to shake all things before the *parousia* (the appearance of Christ at the end of the age)

(1) God's intention to bring humanity into a right relationship with himself through Christ

This declaration of intent is central to the message of the New Testament. Paul says that it was God's intention through Jesus 'to reconcile to himself all things, whether things on earth or things in heaven' (Col 1:20). Paul elaborates this in Romans 8 where he looks forward to the time when 'the creation itself will be liberated from its bondage to decay and brought into the glorious freedom of the children of God' (v 21); and in 2 Corinthians 5:19 he speaks of God reconciling the whole of humanity to himself: 'God was reconciling the world to himself in Christ, not counting men's sins against them.'

It is this divine intention that Paul sometimes refers to as 'a mystery'. In Colossians 2:2 he identifies this 'mystery of God' as being Christ himself, 'in whom are hidden all the treasures of wisdom and knowledge' (v 3). In Ephesians he refers to this mystery a number of times, saying that it has been hidden for ages but 'has now been revealed by the Spirit to God's holy apostles and prophets' (3:5). The mystery which will 'be put into effect when the times have reached their fulfilment' is 'to bring all things in heaven and on earth together under one head, even Christ' (1:10).

This, in effect, is the mystery of the universe, at the heart of which lies the gospel through which it is God's intention to reconcile to himself not only humanity but the whole created order of the physical world. It is in the understanding of this mystery that we are able to perceive meaning and purpose in history. Hence Paul's expansive language of praise to God in Ephesians 1:3–10, not only because of his act of redemption through Christ, but because 'he made known to us the mystery of his will'.

The revelation of God's reconciling purposes, although completed in the New Testament, began in his dealings with his covenant people Israel. Jesus was born into a generation having great expectation that the promises of God would soon be fulfilled. Simeon was said to be 'waiting for the consolation of Israel' (Lk 2:25) and

Anna prophesied over the infant Jesus 'to all who were looking forward to the redemption of Jerusalem' (2:38).

The hope of Israel was for a Redeemer who would be prophet, priest and king. Moses gave this promise to the people before they entered the Promised Land, 'The Lord your God will raise up for you a prophet like me from among your own brothers. You must listen to him' (Deut 18:15). The Redeemer would not simply be a prophet; he would also be a priest. Psalm 110:4 records that God had made this promise by swearing a solemn oath, 'The Lord has sworn and will not change his mind; you are a priest for ever, in the order of Melchizedek.' This promise is dealt with at some length in Hebrews, where the certainty of God's promise is emphasised because priests are not normally appointed with an oath from God. In identifying Jesus with the hope of Israel for a Redeemer-Priest it is noted that through the resurrection Jesus lives for ever so that God has bestowed upon him a permanent priesthood in fulfilment of his promise (Heb 7:24).

Israel's hope for a Redeemer was also that he would be a king. Zechariah 9:9 expresses this as part of the Messianic hope, 'Rejoice greatly, O daughter of Zion! Shout, daughter of Jerusalem! See, your King comes to you, righteous and having salvation.' Jeremiah refers to an everlasting covenant which God had made with David, saying that he would always have a descendant to reign on his throne (Jer 33:19–21). That promise had originally been made through the prophet Nathan who said to David, 'Your house and your kingdom shall endure for ever before me; your throne shall be established for ever' (2 Sam 7:16). The hope of a Redeemer-King after the pattern of David became part of the Messianic hope of Israel which is expressed in Jeremiah 30:8, ' "In that day," declares the Lord Almighty, "I will break the yoke off their necks and will tear off their bonds; no longer will foreigners enslave them. Instead, they will serve the Lord their God and David their king, whom I will raise up for them." '

In the time of Jesus the Messianic hope of Israel was thought to be a human rather than a divine being. Nevertheless, the one who would redeem Israel would be known as 'Immanuel', God with us (Is 7:14) and according to Isaiah 9:6, 'he will be called Wonderful Counsellor, Mighty God, Everlasting Father, Prince of Peace'. Later in Isaiah the one who would redeem Israel is spoken of as the Servant of the Lord (42:1–4) and in 49:5 his mission is defined as 'to bring Jacob back to him and gather Israel to himself'. More importantly, in 53:4–6, there is the recognition that redemption involves suffering. The Redeemer Servant of the Lord actually takes upon himself the sins of the people so that it can be said, 'By his wounds we are healed.' With such a prophecy from one of Israel's foremost prophets it was easy for the apostles of the New Covenant to make the association with Jesus who, before the crucifixion and resurrection, had told them clearly that he would lay down his life of his own accord and that he would 'take it up again' (Jn 10:17–18).

It was an essential part of the witness of the apostles and central to the teaching of the early church that the crucifixion of Jesus was not a random event brought about by the wickedness of men, but was part of the deliberate plan and purpose of God of which Jesus had foreknowledge and which was foretold by the prophets. Paul makes it clear that this was God's own deliberate intention, 'God presented him as a sacrifice of atonement, through faith in his blood' (Rom 3:25) and that the prophets of the old covenant had foreseen this. Thus the atoning death of Christ is declared in the Scriptures, 'For what I received I passed on to you as of first importance: that Christ died for our sins according to the Scriptures' (1 Cor 15:3).

(2) Christ is the centre-point of history

It is the teaching of the New Testament that Christ is shown to be pre-existent, the very agent of creation, who existed before time began. 'Through him,' John says, 'all things are made; without him nothing was made that has been made' (1:3). He has power and authority over all other powers in the universe; 'Having disarmed the powers and authorities, he made a public spectacle of them, triumphing over them by the cross' (Col 2:15). And the day will come when everyone will acknowledge his supremacy. Paul says that God has exalted Christ to the highest place and given him a name above every name, 'That at the name of Jesus every knee should bow, in heaven and on earth and under the earth, and every tongue confess that Jesus Christ is Lord, to the glory of God the Father' (Phil 2:9–11).

H. R. Mackintosh wrote:

Christ is the organ of Creation, absolute in function and eternal in existence; secondly, all things are held together, cohering in that unity and solidarity which makes a cosmos; thirdly, as all things rise in him, so they move on to him as final goal. (H. R. Mackintosh, *The Person of Jesus Christ* [Edinburgh: T. M. T. Clark, 1948], p 70.)

Nicholas Berdyaev noted the significance of the fact that the centrality of Christ in the history of the world is underlined by the fact that we date our calendars around his Advent, numbering the years both forward and backward from the birth of Christ. He says:

The decisive thing is the practice, which has been in vogue only for the last two centuries, of numbering both forward and backward from the birth of Christ. Only when this is done is the Christ event regarded as the temporal mid-point of the entire historical process.

He notes that it is not just Christians who accept this—

but it is the common system in the western world . . . Today
scarcely anyone thinks of the fact that this division is not
merely convention resting upon Christian tradition, but actually presupposes fundamental assertions of New Testament
theology concerning time and history. (Nicholas Berdyaev,
transl. G. Reavey, *The Meaning of History* [London: Geof-
frey Bles, 1936], p 108.)

Even in modern Israel, although they adhere to the Jewish
calendar, they also give dates coinciding with the western
calendar. They do not wish to refer to before and after Christ
so they do not use the symbols BC and AD but they do use
the symbols BCE and CE referring to 'Before the Common
Era' and 'in the Common Era'. In recognising the existence of the Common Era and its dating they are thereby
noting the mid-point in history which is the birth of Jesus!

Similarly, Oscar Cullmann makes the important point
that the difference between the Old Testament understanding of history and that of the New Testament is that the
mid-point of history moves from the future to the past.
The apostles were able to declare that they were witnesses
to the life, death and resurrection of Jesus, but also that he
would come again. Thus, as Cullmann puts it, they were
conscious of living between the mid-point of history and
its culmination in the *parousia* of Christ.

Cullmann uses the illustration of the difference between
D-Day and VE-Day in World War Two. He says that the
first coming of Christ was like D-Day when the most
decisive battles of the war were fought on the Normandy
beaches. Their success guaranteed the enemy's final
defeat, although the war was not in fact finally won for
many months. Christ has already won the decisive battle
through his death and resurrection, but his Second Coming
will be like V-Day when the enemy finally lays down his

arms and surrenders. Thus believers in the Lord Jesus are living in the period between D-Day and V-Day, the First and Second Coming of the Lord Jesus. (Oscar Cullmann, transl. F. V. Filson, *Christ and Time* [Westminster, Philadelphia, 1950], pp 81–84.)

Through this recognition of Christ as the mid-point in history we can gain a clearer understanding, not only of past events and their significance, but also of the future. The New Testament writers regard everything in the past as being fulfilled in Christ, that is, all the promises of God. Christ is the full and final revelation of God. In him we see a reflection of the nature of God and through him we are able to interpret the purposes of God. Those purposes will be completed when he comes again and draws all things together in himself. Paul has a telling passage in Colossians 1:16–17 referring to the centrality of Christ in history. He says, 'For by him all things were created; things in heaven and on earth, visible and invisible, whether thrones or powers or rulers or authorities; all things were created by him and for him. He is before all things and in him all things hold together.' It is notable that Paul refers to the pre-existence of Christ in the present tense, 'He is before all things.'

Anthony Hoekema says:

The Bible teaches us to see human history as completely dominated by Jesus Christ. History is the sphere of God's redemption, in which he triumphs over man's sin through Christ and once again reconciles the world to himself . . . The centrality of Christ in history is symbolically depicted in the fifth chapter of the Book of Revelation. Only the Lamb is worthy to take the scroll and to break its seven seals—the breaking of the seals meaning, not just the interpretation of history, but the execution of the events of history. (A. A. Hoekema, *The Bible and the Future* [Exeter: Paternoster Press, 1979], pp 29–30.)

The New Testament not only sees the centrality of Christ's work of redemption through his first coming, but also looks forward to the culmination of that work in the *parousia* which will be the climax of history. He is therefore able to declare at the end of his own testimony in the final chapter of the last book of the Bible, 'Behold, I am coming soon! My reward is with me, and I will give to everyone according to what he has done. I am the Alpha and the Omega, the first and the last, the beginning and the end' (Rev 22:12–13).

All history looks forward to that final consummation when the purposes of God will be brought to a conclusion through him who was active in creation and in our redemption, and whose advent marks the central point in history.

(3) The kingdom of God

Jesus was born into an age of expectancy. God, who had been active throughout Israel's history, was about to fulfil his promise to send the Messiah-Redeemer. Popular expectation was that the Messiah would liberate the land and the people from the hated Roman overlords. But the Messianic promise linked with the establishment of the New Covenant was, 'I will forgive their wickedness and remember their sins no more' (Jer 31:34). Zechariah had similarly foreseen the role of the Redeemer in the forgiveness of sins. He said, 'On that day a fountain will be opened to the house of David and the inhabitants of Jerusalem, to cleanse them from sin and impurity' (Zech 13:1).

Those who were familiar with the teaching of the Torah and the prophets knew that the forgiveness of sins was a sign of the Messianic age and the presence of the Redeemer. That was why they reacted so angrily when Jesus pronounced the sins of the paralytic man to be forgiven. 'The Pharisees and the teachers of the law began thinking to themselves, "Who is this fellow who speaks blasphemy? Who can forgive sins but God alone?"' (Lk 5:21).

Jesus had begun his ministry with the declaration, 'The time has come, the kingdom of God is near' (Mk 1:15). John the Baptist preached a similar message saying, 'Repent, for the kingdom of heaven is near' (Mt 3:2), but whereas John was looking forward to the one who would come after him and would be more powerful than him, Jesus said, '*The time has come*,' and after reading Isaiah 61 in the synagogue at Nazareth he said, '*Today* this scripture is fulfilled in your hearing' (Lk 4:21). Jesus knew perfectly well that the passage from Isaiah 61, 'The Spirit of the Lord is on me, because he has anointed me to preach good news to the poor . . .'was a prophecy relating to the coming Messiah who would establish the reign of God upon earth. His coming would mark the beginning of a new era; a new age of God's activity in the world which would be clear, not only to Israel, but to the Gentiles, to all the nations. They would see him setting free those who were bound by Satan, opening the eyes of the blind and releasing the oppressed.

Jesus' claim that 'today this scripture is fulfilled' was a clear claim that the new age had already begun. He himself inaugurated the new era which was not to be a kingdom in the territorial sense but was to be the reign of God on earth—the time when God would be dynamically active in the world, carrying out his purpose which he had already revealed to the prophets. That purpose was the redemption of the people from sin and the establishment of new heavens and a new earth.

Jesus, however, knew that this was not the time for the total fulfilment of the purposes of God. The new age was just dawning; its final consummation was still in the future. This is made clear in the discourse recorded by Luke in 17:20–37. When the Pharisees asked Jesus when the kingdom of God would come he replied that it is already here—'The kingdom of God is within you.' But he straightaway went on to say that the work of the kingdom was not yet completed. He himself must first suffer and be rejected, but he would come again at a time when people least expected him. They could be eating, drinking and marrying as in the days of Noah. 'It will be just like this in the day the Son of Man is revealed,' he said (v 30).

At Jesus' Second Coming the nations will be gathered before him for judgement (Mt 25:31f). At his first Advent he did not come to judge the world. Jesus stated this clearly, 'I did not come to judge the world, but to save it' (Jn 12:47). When he came to inaugurate the kingdom he came as Redeemer bringing the good news of God's salvation for all who would accept him: 'For God did not send his Son into the world to condemn the world, but to save the world through him' (Jn 3:17). The *parousia* will bring about the climax of the fulfilment of the purposes of God in the consummation of the kingdom.

Thus the New Testament teaches that the kingdom is a present reality and yet its final fulfilment is still in the future. Its consummation will be at the end of the age with the coming of the Son of Man, but those who accept Jesus immediately enter the kingdom by faith and begin to enjoy its blessings. Those who reject the word of God or who have never heard it remain outside. Although the majority of the world's population is still outside the kingdom this does not make it any less a reality. It is rather like the end of World War Two in the Far East when the Japanese surrendered. Their rule had extended over a huge area of South East Asia. It was an immense task to convey the news of their defeat across this vast territory to reach the scattered population in the remote villages of Burma. There were many people, including Allied soldiers, who did not receive the good news until long after the war was concluded. They were still living under the rule of the enemy without knowing that the new age of freedom had already dawned.

The period between the First and Second Coming of Christ is rather like that. The enemy has already been defeated, although his activity is still present in the world and it will take time to clear up the effects of his actions. He will not be totally destroyed until news of Christ's victory on the cross reaches even the remotest communities. Jesus said the gospel of the kingdom will be preached to all peoples before the end of the age (Mt 24:14). Then he will come again and finally destroy the enemy.

The way to enter the kingdom is through repentance and faith in Jesus. Paul taught that the moment a new believer accepts Christ he enters the kingdom, he is part of the new age, 'He is a new creation' (2 Cor 5:17); but Paul also realised that God had not yet completed the work of the kingdom. There would be a time of judgement and those who deliberately refused to repent and to come into the new relationship with God through Christ were bringing judgement upon themselves. He wrote to the Romans, 'Because of your stubbornness and unrepentant heart, you are storing up wrath against yourself for the day of God's wrath, when his righteous judgement will be revealed' (2:5).

In order to understand the way God is working out his purposes in history it is essential to recognise the nature of the reign of God and to grasp the significance of the kingdom being both present and in the future. This was something that John the Baptist had not perceived at the time of his imprisonment. John had predicted that Jesus would baptise with Holy Spirit and with fire. He declared, 'His winnowing fork is in his hand, and he will clear his threshing-floor, gathering his wheat into the barn and burning up the chaff with unquenchable fire' (Mt 3:12). From the reports he received in prison it was clear that Jesus was indeed gathering the wheat of the harvest into the kingdom but there was no evidence that he was 'burning up the chaff'.

John wanted to see 'the unquenchable fire' of judgement upon the 'brood of vipers' to whom he had preached at the Jordan. He knew them to be an evil generation deserving the wrath of God and he longed to see the one whom he believed to be the Redeemer dealing with them with 'unquenchable fire'; so he sent the message, 'Are you the one who was to come, or should we expect someone else?' (Lk 7:19). Jesus' response was to underline the evidence of the inauguration of the kingdom—the sick healed, evil spirits driven out and the poor hearing the good news. But he did not refer to judgement because that was not the mission of his first Advent.

Up to that point John had not accepted the witness of Jesus so he had not yet entered the new era. Jesus said, 'The one who is least in the kingdom of God is greater than he' (Lk 7:28).

This statement should act as a solemn reminder of the necessity of understanding the strategy as well as the purposes of God. The new age had indeed dawned, as Jesus told the Pharisees, signalled by his power over Beelzebub, 'The kingdom of God has come upon you' (Mt 12:28). Although those who reject the testimony of Jesus put themselves in line for judgement, that judgement does not come upon the nations until the *parousia*. This was Jesus' own teaching, 'There is a judge for the one who rejects me and does not accept my words; that very word which I spoke will condemn him at the last day' (Jn 12:48).

(4) The goal of history

'The last day', to which Jesus referred in John 12:48, is the goal of history, the climax of the activity of God, the time when he will draw all things to a conclusion and finally fulfil his ultimate purposes. This was the unique contribution of the Hebrew prophets. Unlike the Greek philosophers or the sages of any of the nations, the prophets of Israel served a God who held the nations in his hands as a drop in a bucket (Is 40:15). He was the one who sat 'enthroned above the circle of the earth' (Is 40:22). He was the one who 'stretches out the heavens like a canopy . . . He brings princes to nought and reduces the rulers of the world to nothing' (Is 40:22–23).

They revealed a God who was active in the world and who was known by his deeds as well as by his words. So the psalmist was able to say, 'Come and see the works of the Lord' (Ps 46:8) and because everyone in Israel who knew the Lord ought to be able to perceive his activity, Isaiah was able to complain, 'They have no regard for the deeds of the Lord' (Is 5:12).

Since the Hebrew prophets recognised the sovereign control of God, not only over the natural creation, but also over the nations, they were able to declare his word, not only for Israel, but for all the world. From the eighth century onwards there are numerous prophecies directed towards other nations.

Since God was a God of righteousness there would come a time when he would call all the nations of the world to account. The psalmist saw this not simply as a day of judgement, but as a time when God would establish a new era of righteousness upon the earth, 'The Lord reigns for ever; he has established his throne for judgement. He will judge the world in righteousness; he will govern the peoples with justice' (Ps 9:7–8). There are many other passages which speak about God bringing judgement upon the nations such as Isaiah 24, Jeremiah 25, Ezekiel 38, Zephaniah 3, Zechariah 14 and Malachi 4.

The prophecy in Isaiah 65:17f is more far-seeing, going beyond God simply bringing the nations to judgement and foreseeing the time coming when God will establish his reign on earth which will transform the whole created order: 'Behold, I will create new heavens and a new earth.' The prophecy concludes with, 'The wolf and the lamb will feed together, and the lion will eat straw like the ox.' Ezekiel also foresaw the far-reaching consequences of the reign of God. In the vision of the river of life recorded in Ezekiel 47 he saw that wherever the water flowed it transformed the land and made it abundantly fruitful. Even the Dead Sea became filled with life.

This new life, which would be brought about by the reign of God upon earth, featured strongly in Paul's thinking and teaching. The prologue to the letter to the Ephesians is full of praise to the God who has been working out his purposes since before the creation of the world. Those purposes were not only to redeem fallen mankind, adopting them 'as his sons through Jesus Christ' (v 5), but also to redeem the whole cosmos. This, Paul says, is God's intention, 'to be put into effect when the times will have reached their fulfilment—to bring all things in heaven and on earth together under one head, even Christ' (1:10). This same thought is repeated in Colossians 1:20 where Paul emphasises God's intention to reconcile all things to himself.

God's purpose was not only to redeem humanity by presenting believers in Christ 'holy in his sight, without blemish and free from accusation' (Col 1:22) but also to extend that redemption to the whole of creation. 'The creation itself will be liberated from its bondage to decay and brought into the glorious freedom of the children of

God' (Rom 8:21). Paul saw the whole of creation waiting with eager expectation for the final consummation of God's purposes (Rom 8:19). Man's fall into sin had not only affected humanity, but the whole of God's creation, therefore God would extend his redemption to the whole physical universe. The final act of the divine drama would be to restore creation to its original harmony where even the wild animals would live at peace with one another.

This is the biblical revelation of the goal of history. For the New Testament writers this included the Second Coming of Christ, the general resurrection, the day of judgement and the new heavens and new earth. The new heavens and new earth are shown as the climax and culmination of God's activity in creation and re-creation. We may therefore conclude that the whole of history is moving towards this goal.

It is this biblical revelation of the climax of world events which gives meaning to history. It is this understanding of the meaning of history which has been largely lost by the twentieth-century church. It is not a teaching that is being emphasised in the writings of biblical theologians and it is not something that is frequently heard on the lips of preachers. Without this understanding of the activity of God in world events, history has no meaning and the nations are simply seen as being driven helplessly by the secular forces of social change. As a consequence of this lack of biblical understanding of the purposes of God, church leaders give an uncertain sound and church polity lacks direction and a clear sense of purpose. Thus the church also is being driven by the forces of change in the same way as politicians and secularists. There is an urgent need for the church to move from being retroactive to being pro-active. But this will only happen as the church recovers the biblical understanding of the God of history and the way he is working out his purposes in the world today.

(5) The strategy of God

God does not want his people to remain in ignorance, being driven helplessly like a rudderless ship in a storm at the mercy of wind and waves. The biblical revelation of the purposes of God also gives us glimpses of the strategy God uses to accomplish his will. The prophet Haggai has an important word about a time coming when God will shake the nations and the whole created order. He says, 'This is what the Lord Almighty says: "In a little while I will once more shake the heavens and the earth, the sea and the dry land. I will shake all nations, and the desired of all nations will come, and I will fill this house with glory," says the Lord Almighty' (Hag 2:6–7).

Clearly Haggai expected some great cosmic event to be initiated by God in the near future. He sent a message to the governor of Judah, Zerubbabel, reporting God saying, 'I will shake the heavens and the earth. I will overturn royal thrones and shatter the power of foreign kingdoms' (Hag 2:21–22). He foresaw a time of chaos and confusion resulting in those on the same side killing each other in the disarray and turmoil of battle. But the prophecy in verses 6 and 7 has wider implications, referring to the shaking of all nations and a cosmic upheaval shaking the heavens as well as everything on earth.

This global shaking does not appear connected with the more localised and immediate shaking envisaged in the message to Zerubbabel. A further significant fact is that it links the shaking with the time of international spiritual harvest. The prophet saw God drawing those who would respond in *all nations* and bringing them into his household which would be filled with the glory of his presence.

It is perhaps of even greater significance that this prophecy is repeated in Hebrews 12 from verse 26. The context makes it clear that the writer regards this prophecy as being linked with the reign of God upon earth, the kingdom inaugurated by Jesus but yet awaiting final consummation. Referring to the shaking of the earth and the heavens he says, 'The words "once more" indicate the removing of what can be shaken—that is, created things— so that what cannot be shaken may remain. Therefore, since we are receiving a kingdom that cannot be shaken, let us be thankful . . .'

The double explanation here gives both the reason for the shaking and its timing. The interpretation given is that God's strategy is to create a separation between material things which are temporary in nature and spiritual things which are eternal. He links this with the coming of the kingdom, which gives it an additional link with Haggai's prophecy where shaking and spiritual harvest are brought together.

There are numerous other passages in Scripture referring to God's activity in shaking the earth, the nations and individuals. Isaiah 2:19–21 twice uses the phrase 'when he rises to shake the earth'. This is part of a longer prophecy foreseeing a time coming when God would deal with the pride and arrogance of man. 'The Lord Almighty has a day in store for all the proud and lofty' (v 12). The objective of the shaking is that 'the Lord alone will be exalted in that day' (v 17).

Jesus also refers to the time coming when there will be a cosmic shaking: 'The stars will fall from the sky, and heavenly bodies will be shaken' (Mt 24:29; Mk 13:25). This statement draws heavily upon similar pronouncements in Isaiah 13:10, 34:4 and Joel 2:31. Each of these Old Testament prophecies is connected with a day of the Lord and it is in that context that Jesus uses them. He is looking forward to the *parousia*, the climax of history and divine intervention in human affairs—in other words the final consummation of the kingdom which he inaugurated.

5

Global Shaking

In a little while I will once more shake the heavens and the earth, the sea and the dry land (Hag 2:6).

The twentieth century, which has witnessed the greatest period of scientific and technological change in history, has also experienced an unprecedented escalation in the destabilising forces of social, economic and political change which have affected every region of the world. Fundamental questions are: Does God have any hand in the forces of change sweeping across the globe? Is humanity being driven helplessly by impersonal forces of change which scientific and social analysts see as gathering a momentum of their own, largely beyond human control? If the forces of change are beyond the power of humanity to control, are they conforming to any divine pattern or are they also beyond God's power to control?

It is in the face of such fundamental questions at what, in the view of secular humanists, is a critical period in the history of the planet, that we need to draw upon our knowledge of the nature and purposes of God.

We have already made the point that the Bible reveals God as one who is active rather than a passive impersonal force. God's activity can be seen both in the natural creation and in human affairs at both a global and an individual level.

Chapters 40–45 in Isaiah contain a revelation of God that is fundamental to an understanding of his activity in the world and therefore to any interpretation of contemporary history. He is revealed as active in creation and in international affairs. He is the one who has measured the waters in the hollow of his hand, marked off the heavens, weighed the mountains on scales and stretched out the heavens like a canopy. It was he who created the heavens and the earth, who holds the nations like a drop in a bucket, who reduces the rulers of the world to nothing. He is the first and the last, apart from him there is no God; he formed the light and created darkness, he brings prosperity and creates disaster. He is able to 'anoint' Cyrus the Persian emperor who did not even know the name of the Lord and use him to subdue nations, to release the people of Israel and Judah from captivity and to rebuild Jerusalem.

This biblical revelation of God does not limit the freedom of men and women to act according to their own choice. It does, however, emphasise the fact that, despite the presence of sin in the world and the deliberate wickedness of individuals and whole people groups who oppose the good, righteous and just purposes of God, he steadily accomplishes his purposes from generation to generation. This provides us with the key to understanding the mystery of the universe. It gives us an understanding of history which gives meaning and purpose to life.

In this chapter we shall be looking at some of the events of the twentieth century and seeking to understand their significance as part of the processes of change which are moving the world towards the final goal of history. It is important to remember that not everything that happens is initiated by God or is in accord with his desire for the nations or for individual lives. It was certainly not his desire that there should be two world wars during the past century or that millions of people should suffer and die from persecution or famine or other disasters. This would conflict with the biblical revelation of the nature of God as a God of love who is compassionate and merciful and who longs for all people to know him and to be in a right relationship with him, which is his ultimate purpose.

But although many things happen which are not God's desire, he never loses absolute control. He ensures that all things do eventually work together to work out his purposes. He rarely intervenes directly in human affairs to influence the course of history. Usually he allows the nations to take their course, continuing to communicate his unchanging word through the Bible and through those of his servants in every generation who are listening to him and seeking to understand the application of his word to contemporary events. He awaits the moment when individuals and nations are receptive to his word so that he may advance his purposes.

A major part of God's strategy today is to shake humanity's confidence in its own ability to direct the affairs of the nations through human technology, power and intellect. The destabilising forces which have been gaining momentum throughout the twentieth century are achieving this, leaving even the most powerful rulers with the feeling of powerlessness as political and economic forces sweep away the old structures, bringing down mighty rulers and changing the map of the world.

The natural order

One of the ways in which the world is being shaken today is through natural disasters which have been occurring with increasing frequency, especially in the second half of the twentieth century. These natural disasters have included earthquakes, hurricanes, floods, droughts, famines and plagues. There is statistical evidence showing the increasing frequency of occurrence and severity of natural disasters. Yet this in itself is not a major factor in the shaking of the nations.

Most of these disasters, although widely reported in the news media, only make a significant impact in a local or regional area. Western news media give very little coverage to disasters occurring in the poorer parts of the world. An earthquake in China, killing 600 people, is given barely a mention in the foreign news pages of the broadsheets.

By contrast, the 1993 Los Angeles earthquake which killed no one but destroyed a lot of property in downtown LA was given massive coverage. The media, however, scrupulously avoided reporting that the epicentre of the quake was right on the location of the area producing nine-tenths of California's pornographic films and videos. The largest of the video producers lost all its master tapes. At a single blow California's pornographic video industry was virtually wiped out. But this was not the kind of news the media like to report in case anybody should hint at divine judgement! The one thing the secular media cannot tolerate is any suggestion that God is active in human history!

Most of the natural disasters in recent years have only been disasters because of the human element in them. They have either been contributed to by human activity or they were preventable. The big quakes of the 1980s which caused much loss of life, such as East Turkey October 1983, Mexico City September 1985 and Armenia December 1988, were all contributed to by shoddy buildings erected on areas of known earthquake activity. The 1983 East Turkey earthquake which killed 2,000 was in the same area where 4,000 had died in a quake only seven years earlier.

The recurring floods in Bangladesh and north-east India, such as that in October 1988 which killed thousands and left twenty million people homeless, was contributed to by the destruction of the forests up in the Himalayas where half the forest reserves were lost between 1950 and 1980. This caused a tremendous increase in soil erosion which was carried down the Ganges and Brahma Putra rivers hundreds of miles away causing silting which aggravated the flooding.

A spectacular example of humanly created natural disaster occurred in the Soviet Union in the 1950s. The authorities attempted to boost agricultural output in the central Asian republics by diverting water from two great rivers which flowed into the Aral Sea. It appeared to be a wonderful success. It boosted crops, cotton, rice, fruit and vegetables through a massive irrigation programme. But thirty years later the Aral Sea had virtually disappeared, with the once thriving coastal towns of Aralsk and Muinak left high and dry, their fishing grounds transformed into a salty desert.

Hundreds more examples could be given of the way human activity in the twentieth century has created the conditions for, or contributed to, many natural disasters. The most obvious of these is that of pollution.

Pollution is not a new problem, although it is associated with modernisation. The Industrial Revolution produced numerous urban communities throughout Europe living in grimy, unhealthy conditions with poor sanitation and a lack of clean water, but above all breathing in air laden with industrial fumes. These minor ecological disasters were, however, localised. They did not affect the rich owners of industry or the decision-makers who lived well away from the polluted areas.

London is a prime example of this, where the social geography was formed by the climate. The East End of London has always been a working-class community whereas the West End has always been home to the rich. In the early days of the Industrial Revolution a variety of industry grew up around the East London docks. It included the chemical plants of Silvertown and the smelly glue factories of Stratford. The prevailing westerly winds over London carried the smells away from the entrepreneurs and owners of industry west of the city, enabling them to live in comfort.

The twentieth century has transformed the urban industrial scene to such an extent that what was once a local problem has now become global. The expansion of industry and urbanisation in Britain caused the smogs familiar to Londoners in the late nineteenth century and early twentieth century. In one week of December 1873 700 people died in a great London smog. Even so, no action was taken until 1952 when smog killed 4,000 people in London alone and left tens of thousands ill with respiratory problems. This caused the government to pass the Clean Air Act of 1954 which has meant that smog in Britain is now virtually unknown. This demonstrates clearly man's ability to control environmental damage where there is both the will and the resources.

The poorer nations are powerless to deal with environmental problems of the massive scale now confronting them due to the population explosion taking place in many parts of the world. Since 1950 economies in the western industrialised nations have grown considerably and average wealth is much higher, whereas economic activity has actually reduced in sub-Sahara Africa and people are significantly poorer. According to the World Watch Institute (quoted in Paul Kennedy, *Preparing for the Twenty-First Century* [London: Harper Collins, 1993], p 98) there was more livestock than people in sub-Sahara Africa in 1950 but today the position is reversed. The population has more than doubled in that time but the increase in livestock has not kept pace. The problem is caused by over-grazing and soil erosion which reinforces the 'cycle of ecological degradation and deepening human poverty'.

The massive growth in cities throughout the world and increasing industrialisation, together with the destruction of the rain forests, over-fishing the seas, poisoning the atmosphere and pollution of land and rivers, is creating global problems which are causing grave anxieties in most parts of the world. These problems are no longer localised but are worldwide. No one really knows how serious they are for the future of the planet. The so-called 'greenhouse effect' or 'global warming' appears an insoluble problem which is intensifying as the world's population continues to explode.

The earth is basically a closed system surrounded by a thin layer of atmosphere which is uniquely balanced to allow a certain amount of the sun's rays to enter, giving warmth and light essential to life and healthy growth. The unique balance of gases within the earth's atmosphere enables just the right amount of the sun's radiant energy to penetrate while radiating back into space the surplus energy.

But if—as scientists now believe is happening—the composition of the trace gases in our atmosphere is altered by human activity, then more re-radiated heat is being "trapped" (as within the glass of a greenhouse), which not only warms up the atmospheric gases but everything else as well. At the same time, scientists are also concerned that the ozone layer, which protects the earth and its inhabitants from harmful solar radiation, is being significantly depleted by chemical emissions like CFCs. The wider the "ozone hole", whether it be over Antarctica or New England, the more vulnerable human beings are, say, to skin cancer. (Paul Kennedy, *Ibid*, p 106.)

The clearing and burning of forests, the use of great amounts of coal, oil and natural gases, plus the pollution from factories and cities with millions of vehicles on the roads, is significantly increasing the amount of carbon dioxide in the atmosphere. As this increases, the earth's temperature gradually rises. Scientists predict that carbon dioxide levels will be so high by the middle of the twenty-first century that this will lead to significant rises in the earth's average temperature. This in turn will cause dramatic changes to the functioning of the whole global ecosystem.

No one really knows what effect these changes will have upon agriculture, fertility, or the weather systems around the earth, but one thing is certain and that is that sea levels will rise as the ice in the Arctic and Antarctic regions melts. The United Nations has already compiled a list of ten countries most vulnerable to flooding in the next half century.

Higher temperatures will also create a greater demand for water and dry up lakes and reservoirs, reducing soil moisture with the consequent decline in agricultural yields. Thus food production is likely to fall at the same time as the world's population continues to grow at an alarming rate. All the indications are that mankind is heading for a natural disaster of unimaginable proportions.

The natural order of creation is indeed being shaken but the warning signs are clear and if they are heeded the disaster need not occur. In order to save the planet from destruction we have first to respect it as a precious resource given to us by God as a perfect creation. Drastic changes in our lifestyle are required, especially the curbing of greed and exploitation. The greatest responsibility lies with the rich industrialised nations where only one-fifth of the world's population live but they consume more than two-thirds of the world's natural resources. How soon will the rich recognise the danger and be shaken out of their blind complacency?

Economic systems

The second half of the twentieth century has seen a phenomenal expansion of the world economy which is the result of a number of interrelated causes. After World War Two the major trading nations set up a system to restrict protectionist tendencies and to encourage financial and economic stability. The General Agreement on Trade and Tariffs (GATT), plus regular contact between the finance ministers of the seven most powerful industrialised nations, backed by institutions such as the World Bank, have not only contributed to a measure of international economic stability but have materially increased general prosperity. Since 1945 the global economy has grown more than in the whole of world history prior to World War Two. Global GMT quadrupled from two trillion to eight trillion US dollars between 1950 and 1980.

Despite this tremendous increase in industrial productivity, the service industries such as advertising, banking and insurance, plus increased agricultural production and a massive increase in international trade, the gap between the rich nations and the poor nations has not been bridged. On the contrary, it has widened. Thus the increase in the creation and enjoyment of wealth has served to raise living standards in the rich industrialised nations but the gap between the 'haves' and 'have nots' has appreciably widened. For example, in 1991 the per capita gross domestic product of Switzerland was 36,300 dollars,

Sweden was 32,600, Japan 29,000 dollars; but India's per capita GDP was only 360 dollars and Nigeria's a mere 278 dollars. Additionally, there are many more poor nations in Africa and Asia with even lower average per capita GDPs. After half a century of unprecedented global economic growth the world still has more than one billion people living in absolute poverty.

One of the major economic developments of the second half of the twentieth century which has contributed considerably to economic growth is the development of multinational corporations. This corporate globalisation has increased at such a spectacular rate of growth that it is quite possible that in the foreseeable future there will be no national industries and no identifiable national products or specifically national technologies.

For countries such as Britain, with its island mentality and its history of being in the forefront of industrial development and for so long the world's leading economic power, the idea of losing all its national industries and commercial institutions is as hard to swallow as the loss of the British Empire and its former position as the leading maritime nation in the world. The United States is similarly going through a period of revolutionary economic change as the gradual removal of trade barriers and the development of multi-national corporations increasingly draws foreign investment into the US, particularly from Japan.

Another major development in the past half century has been the globalisation of financial markets which have experienced an unprecedented boom due to the deregulation of world money markets and the revolutionary new technologies in global communications. Ninety per cent of money exchanged today is not related to the sale of goods. These global financial transactions, shifting money from one currency to another and entrepreneurial dealings on the Stock Market, take place twenty-four hours a day as the major exchanges open and close around the world passing information instantly from one computer screen to the next.

One result of this globalisation of economic forces is the diminishing ability of national governments to exercise control over their own economies. In recent years we have seen the power of currency speculators to influence interest rates and even to cause the devaluation of a particular currency. National loyalty or patriotism plays no part in the lives of currency speculators whose only concern is to make vast sums of money. This was well illustrated in the September 1992 'Black Wednesday' which forced the devaluation of the pound when British dealers on the London currency market were shouting, 'Kill sterling!' One would hardly have thought that these were British bankers eagerly participating in a gigantic gamble to harm their own country's economy.

This lack of national loyalty is also a feature of the development of multi-national corporations where the chief concern is with the maximisation of profits. The multi-nationals are in deadly competition with their rivals and are constantly seeking new markets and fresh locations where their production costs will be lower. The 1990s have seen a significant development in this with Japanese cars being produced in Malaysia and other multi-nationals moving into the Philippines, Indonesia and other developing nations where cheap labour is available. This has the effect of raising levels of unemployment and reducing economic prosperity in those rich nations which spawned the multi-nationals. This is no concern of the directors of the multi-nationals so long as profits continue to rise. The social consequences of their moving production bases, taking over other industries or changing their distribution networks are of no concern. Their primary objective is the maximisation of profit and the elimination of competitors.

The growth of the global marketplace is having significant political and social impact. It means that no one is in control except the directors of corporations who are responsible, not to governments, but to their shareholders. Greed is the driving force behind the global economy today. It is a force which governments are powerless to control. It is beginning to sweep across the globe with increasing ferocity. The genie of human greed has been loosed from the bottle and humanity is powerless to put it back. The gap between the rich and poor nations is increasing; but so too is the gap between the 'haves' and 'have nots' within the rich nations. Thus levels of relative deprivation are rising to dangerous levels.

Those who are deprived know that the rich are enjoying untold luxury because this is constantly being communicated to them through television and global communications networks. There comes a point when those who are deprived will no longer tolerate the injustice that forces them to live in poverty while others enjoy untold wealth. Attitudes harden and become the seed of revolution. The clamour from the world's poor, the demands for justice, may well become intolerable in the early years of the twenty-first century as the international corporations extend their control over the nations. The world's economies are rapidly becoming a battleground, even using the language of war, as the multi-nationals seek to eliminate each other and the boardroom battles for power escalate towards the day when a mere handful of men will control the whole global economic systems.

This is a scene strikingly similar to that depicted in the Book of Revelation where the control of the world's economy means that no one can buy or sell without submitting to the authority of the world dictator: 'He also forced everyone, small or great, rich or poor, free and slave, to receive a mark on his right hand or on his forehead, so that no-one could buy or sell unless he had the mark' (Rev 13:16–17). Global economic trends are moving in the direction whereby that prophecy can be fulfilled in the not-too-distant future.

The rise of the multi-nationals has in some ways had a stabilising effect upon the world economy since national and regional fluctuations in commodity and share prices can be ironed out by the greater spread of the big corporations. But nothing was able to save the market from the biggest plunge of the century which became known as 'Black Monday', 19th October 1987. Fifty billion pounds, or ten per cent, was wiped off the value of publicly quoted companies in London alone. The fall in Wall Street was more than double the London figure, wiping 22.5 per cent off share values, which was twice the drop on the worst day of the great crash in October 1929. The whole economic system of the western capitalist world was profoundly shaken on that day.

Analysts have spent a great deal of energy in trying to assess the causes of the 1987 Market crash which followed five years of steady gains. The usual explanation given is that shares were over-valued and the Market was simply correcting itself. There was, however, another factor which the secular analysts overlooked—that is, its connection with events a few days earlier.

In the early hours of the morning of Friday, 16th October 1987 a hurricane-force wind swept across the coast of south-east England with winds of 110 miles an hour, causing greater havoc than any other storm this century. It was in fact the strongest storm to hit England since the hurricane of 1703, the year John Wesley was born. Although there was little loss of life, due to most people being in bed, there was immense damage to property and some sixteen million trees were destroyed, including a third of Kew Gardens' rare trees and six out of the seven oaks in the Kentish town of that name. Roads and rail links throughout London and the south-east were blocked, telephone lines were down and electricity was cut off in much of the region for the first time since World War Two.

For the first time in its history the London Stock Exchange failed to open. Workers were simply unable to get into the capital. The City of London, still the most influential financial centre in the world, with more than twice as many international banks located in the square mile than in New York, was virtually closed down. During the day there had been some selling in Tokyo and small falls in New York. If London had been open on that Friday it is very possible that it would have exercised a steadying influence upon the Market.

The London Market reopened on Monday, 19th October after a miserable weekend clearing up from the ravages of storm damage. People struggled into work in the City of London through a trail of damage, with roofs torn off, trees strewn across the countryside, crushed cars and power lines still down. A mood of depression hung over the City and, seeing the slight falls on Wall Street, traders began selling. When the American market opened a few hours later the London Market was selling briskly. Immediately Wall Street took a nosedive. In the first hour-and-a-half the Dow Jones fell 200 points. By the end of the day it was down from 2,250 to 1,725.

Clear prophetic warnings had been published in the magazine *Prophecy Today* throughout that year that the great shaking of the rich industrialised nations was about to begin and that before the end of the year there would be a major financial crash. The shaking would be aimed at the capitalist economic system which was the source of their power and pride.

For Britain 1987 was a year of significant events which began with the sinking of the cross-channel ferry 'Herald of Free Enterprise' with the loss of 187 lives. In August a gunman went on the rampage in the quiet Berkshire town of Hungerford killing fourteen and leaving fifteen wounded while he acted out occult-inspired war games. October saw the hurricane bring devastation to the most affluent area of Britain followed by the Stock Market crash. The following month there was one of the worst atrocities in the twenty-five years of troubles in Ulster when the IRA blew up a crowd attending an open-air Remembrance Day service in Enniskillen. This was followed two weeks later by the worst disaster on the London Underground with a fireball inferno at King's Cross station which killed thirty people.

The great shaking had begun. Britain had experienced an unprecedented string of intense disasters; confidence in the new globalised economy was waning; and the world began to plunge towards the deepest and longest recession of the century.

Was the hand of God to be seen in all this? While we can see here that the storm was a factor in triggering the Stock Market crash, there is plenty of other evidence of a link between events in the natural order of creation and the economic problems of the late twentieth century. The most outstanding example is problems in the insurance world.

The succession of manmade and natural disasters which shook the world through the 1980s resulted in massive insurance claims. It is of course impossible to predict the number of storms, hurricanes, earthquakes and floods which will occur in a given period, but insurers through-out the western world grossly under-estimated the number of natural disasters and the size of the huge financial claims that would be made. Many of the world's insurers re-insure with Lloyds of London to offset their liabilities so that, as the claims for compensation grew, a near panic situation was created in Lloyds in the early 1990s as underwriters struggled to meet their guaranteed indemnity, especially those where natural disasters had hit western nations. They were still dealing with the claims of the 1980s while they viewed with dismay the relentless series of disasters still occurring in the 1990s, such as the San Francisco and Los Angeles earthquakes and the great floods of the Mississippi/Missouri rivers in the USA.

The shaking of Lloyds of London was so severe that it even put a question mark over its survival as a financial institution, but it also had a devastating effect upon the lives of thousands of Lloyds Names. These are the people who put their personal assets at risk through the underwriters to guarantee payment of claims. For years they had benefited from a steady stream of profits through the system, but suddenly they were called upon to pay out rather than receive. The rich and the powerful throughout Britain were shaken. Many were forced to sell shares or lost their lifetime savings; others were forced to sell their London flats or country homes and some even committed suicide as a result of the hopeless position in which they found themselves. The housing market was flooded with beautiful mansions which further depressed the housing market and affected confidence in the economy.

Many of the rich and powerful in Britain who had enjoyed comfortable lifestyles and thought they had financial security for life were rudely shaken and forced to change their lifestyle, but above all they lost confidence in the material securities which they had once taken for granted and which played such an important part in their lives.

Was this part of God's intention? Did he deliberately plan the natural disasters as part of the shaking of the nations? There is certainly evidence to support such a belief; but God does not have to initiate directly many of the things which contribute to the fulfilling of his declared intentions. He simply has to await the sinful, greedy actions of mankind to bring about their own inevitable consequences. Those who ignore the word of the Lord and pursue their own evil intentions eventually reap the appropriate reward.

The truth of this statement was vividly illustrated by the collapse of the London-based merchant bankers, Baring Brothers, in February 1995. It soon became evident that there was a connection with the Kobe earthquake which had rocked Japan a month earlier. The trader at the heart of Baring's troubles had been betting that the Japanese market would rise, whereas the earthquake caused a fall in share prices. *The Independent* newspaper noted this and said that Baring Brothers had been humbled by 'an act of God'. *The Independent* does not have a reputation for paying much respect to God, so they were no doubt saying this with tongue in cheek. But it is nevertheless a fact that there was a direct connection between the earthquake and the bank's troubles.

The Baring Brothers crash exposed things that the Bible says are hated by God, namely greed, lies and deceit. Yet the financial practices being carried out by Barings that led to bankruptcy are common in many other financial institutions. It is, however, doubtful if they have taken notice of the warning signs, because greed drives men to take whatever risks they think necessary to achieve their objectives. So long as there are one or two players left in the market they will continue to gamble, no doubt hoping they will be the only one to survive and thereby corner the market and gain maximum profits.

At the same time as Baring Brothers was hitting the world headlines, the US Congress was struggling to fix its national budget. In the event it only succeeded in agreeing to yet another $200 billion deficit to add to the debt mountain which included more than $800 billion owed to other nations. The interest paid on this was greater than the entire annual US defence budget. As the world's largest debtor nation the USA has, since the late 1980s, been plunging deeper into debt—a situation which clearly cannot continue for ever. No nation can go on spending more than it earns, and the day of reckoning will surely come.

The day will come when, not only banks, but powerful nations will also become bankrupt as a direct result of the greed, aggression, lies and deceit which are driving the world's economy. These are destructive forces which are gathering momentum and will not simply have economic consequences; they will also trigger unprecedented social upheavals. These will come about as a result of the development of global capitalism which continually seeks to maximise profits irrespective of social consequences. Multi-national corporations will continue relentlessly seeking to shift their production bases into countries where labour is cheap. The Japanese have been doing this for some years but the process was greatly stimulated by the twenty per cent surge in the value of the yen against the dollar in the first quarter of 1995. This had a seriously damaging effect upon the Japanese economy as it meant that goods produced at home were being priced out of the world market. Japan is surrounded by poor nations with unlimited cheap labour such as Malaysia, Thailand, the Philippines and Indonesia. But the social consequences of Japanese corporations building factories in these countries may well prove to be disastrous for Japan with rising unemployment among people used to high standards of living.

A similar situation exists in Europe where Germany is

the major economic engine and the strength of the mark presents a similar threat to rising prosperity. Europeans will also be forced to seek cheaper production bases in the face of Japan's off-shore economic drive. The difficulty for the Europeans is where to seek such bases. Africa and the Middle East are too unstable. Eastern Europe would appear to be the answer but this too will have long-term political and social consequences which will threaten the stability of the European Union. The social consequences in western Europe of rising levels of long-term unemployment may well prove to be catastrophic. The rich western nations have grown used to affluence and regard material prosperity as a right. With growing levels of aggression and violent crime a breakdown of law and order on a revolutionary scale in Europe, Japan and America is all too possible early in the twenty-first century.

The downfall of western civilisation is not only a distinct possibility—it is the inevitable consequence of the destructive forces which have been loosed into the world through the wilful greed and wickedness of mankind. In plain biblical terms, the nations are under judgement. Their economic endeavours, central to their pride and wealth, will also be the means of their downfall. All the warning signs have been ignored. The rich nations plunge blindly on towards destruction.

Two words from Isaiah have a powerful message on this issue:

> 'Woe to the obstinate children,' declares the Lord, 'to those who carry out plans that are not mine' (Is 30:1).

> This is the plan determined for the whole world; this is the hand stretched out over all nations. For the Lord Almighty has purposed, and who can thwart him? His hand is stretched out, and who can turn it back? (Is 14:26–27).

6

Shaking the Nations

'I will shake all nations, and the desired of all nations will come, and I will fill this house with glory,' says the Lord Almighty (Hag 2:7).

We have already referred to the radical changes which have taken place throughout the world during the twentieth century which have transformed the political geography of the world since 1900. This has been a century of war, revolution and bloodshed which has been aided and abetted by scientific discovery and technological advances which have produced new and more horrifying weapons of destruction. The gas used in the trench warfare of World War One, which left thousands of men damaged for life and caused a major outcry against the perpetrators, seems mild compared with the fearful array of weaponry available today. The horrors of international chemical and bio-chemical warfare have not actually taken place but their threat hangs like a cloud over mankind.

The 1990s witnessed the end of the Cold War and the great division of the world into East and West which for forty years had presented a constant threat of a nuclear holocaust engulfing half the world. Strangely enough, that division, with its threat of mutual extinction, actually

97

contributed to a degree of stability in the world throughout the Cold War period.

With the collapse of the Soviet Union the old stable structures of the international political scene began to crumble, and with these instabilities and uncertainties there came new threats. The crumbling military-industrial complex of the former USSR threw tens of thousands of nuclear scientists and technicians into unemployment or vastly reduced circumstances. They had once occupied some of the most privileged occupations in the old Soviet Union but now they were unwanted. With the whole economy of the country in turmoil some of them were sufficiently disaffected to sell their skills or their products to anyone offering them hard currency.

Suspicion that this was happening was confirmed in August 1994 when German customs officials intercepted a Spanish businessman travelling from Moscow with a lead-lined suitcase full of enriched plutonium of sufficient quality, although not quantity, to make an atomic bomb. Investigation traced the source to Russian atomic energy plants and fears were confirmed that Russian laboratories were leaking highly dangerous materials into the hands of international criminals.

The fear that nuclear weapons could be developed by smaller unstable nations, or fall into the hands of international terrorist organisations, was suddenly transformed from the realm of science fiction to reality. The shaking of the nations which undermined the old stable political structures brought with it a whole new dimension of fear which threatened the future of humanity.

In order to understand the significance of the major political changes which have occurred during the twentieth century they need to be seen alongside the economic changes and technological developments which have taken place. We have seen that there has been a process of economic globalisation due to the application of advanced technology to communications and information storage systems, plus the growth of multi-national corporations. This economic change has been accompanied by a movement towards the centralisation of power in international politics. When we look at this alongside the collapse of world empires which has taken place during the twentieth century it sounds like a contradictory statement. But what we are noting is underlying trends, or forces of change which are at work, rather than the *phenomenology* of change.

Look at the facts of political change. Numerous great empires have disappeared during the twentieth century; the Prussian Empire, the Hapsburg, the British Empire, the French, the Dutch, Portuguese and Spanish Empires, the Empire of the Chinese Ming Dynasty, the Japanese Empire, the Communist Empire of the USSR and Eastern Europe, and even the white man's empire of South Africa. Most of these empires were built on exploitation and injustice; they were maintained by subjection and the force of arms. Their downfall has largely been brought about by the irrepressible longing for freedom among subject peoples which has given rise to a wave of nationalism sweeping across the world during the second half of the twentieth century.

This has brought about the creation of many new states on the continent of Africa, in the Middle East and also in Asia. Most of these nation states have been born out of the womb of colonialism whereby the former European overlords fixed the territorial boundaries. These boundaries took little or no notice of people groups or tribal associations. Historically they have given rise to untold conflicts within the newly independent nations such as the civil war between north and south in Nigeria, and similar conflicts between north and south in Ethiopia and the Sudan. All three of these had a strong element of religious as well as tribal conflict involving a clash of Muslim and Christian groups.

The same aspirations for autonomy among people groups have been seen in Europe since the collapse of Communism. This resulted in the division of Czechoslovakia and the break-up of the former Yugoslavia, with the indescribable atrocities between the Serbs, Croats and Bosnian Muslims. These local conflicts have been seen by many as a reversion to tribalism. But in fact it is not so much a reversion to old tribal loyalties but a reaction to the forces of globalisation which are sweeping across the world. This return to roots reflects modern man's search for an identity in a world where the individual has less and less significance. It reflects his longing to be part of a small group where the individual has significance and where there is support for one another within a community; where each one belongs and draws security and personal identity from within the group.

In a very real sense this hunger for belongingness and personal identity gives great opportunity for the gospel. This must be reckoned as one of the reasons why there has been such a worldwide growth of the church in the second half of the twentieth century. This growth has coincided with the demand for independence, the breakdown of colonialism and the emergence of new nation states. It is within many of these new states that there has been an explosion of evangelism, commitment to Christ and growth of the church.

This church growth in the developing nations has had to take place in the context of the desire for freedom from colonial powers, which has led to fundamental changes in the policy of missionary societies and western-orientated churches. The practice of indigenisation has become standard since the middle of the century, resulting in the withdrawal of western missionaries, the training of local leadership within the mainline churches as well as the formation of numerous indigenous churches.

We return now to the question of globalisation in the economy and the drive towards the centralisation of political power on the international scene. Despite all the appearances to the contrary, the underlying political forces which have been gathering momentum during the second half of the twentieth century will eventually centralise political power and take over the role of the nation state. Indeed, we may expect to see the disappearance of the nation state during the twenty-first century. This sounds highly improbable but in fact the world is being driven by forces of change which are beyond the control of individual nations. As these forces of change progress they are raising issues which are beyond the ability of national governments to solve.

Paul Kennedy, writing on these issues, says:

These various trends, from global warming to twenty-four hour a day trading, are trans-national by nature, crossing borders all over the globe, affecting distant societies, and reminding us that the earth, for all its divisions, is a single unit. They are largely out of the control of the authorities of the traditional nation state, both in the direct sense that countries cannot prevent incoming atmospheric drift and in the indirect sense that if they banned such activities as biotech farming, robotics, and foreign exchange dealing, that would not stop them operating elsewhere. Finally, these challenges cannot be met by military force, which is the normal way states have handled threats to their security. Carrier task forces and armoured divisions have their uses, but they are unable to prevent the global demographic explosion, stop the greenhouse effect, halt foreign exchange dealings, ban automated factories and biotech farming in foreign countries, and so on. (*Ibid*, p 129.)

Many observers of the international scene are recognising that the issues confronting humanity in the twenty-first century are global and they therefore require global rather than national policies. These can only be achieved either by a unique formula of international co-operation or by the centralisation of authority vested in some international institution. The seeds of this international authority have already been sown in the boost given to the United Nations in having to deal with Saddam Hussein's invasion of Kuwait. The UN raised an army to fight the Gulf War and there have been many calls since then for a standing UN controlled army to act as an international security force dealing with localised conflicts which threaten the security of others either on a regional or global basis. Such an armed force could also be employed to deal with the growing threat of international terrorist organisations and the international drugs network.

These demands for a central authority are likely to grow as the world plunges at an ever-increasing pace into the twenty-first century and discovers that the old ways of international diplomacy and attempts to harness the efforts of nation states in a single direction simply do not work or are insufficient to deal with the new global issues which threaten the security, and indeed the very existence of life upon the planet.

These political forces of change gathering momentum in the world move the nations a step closer towards the scenario envisioned in Revelation 13 where it is foreseen that there will be a one-world economy, controlled by a one-world government and enforcing a one-world religion. These three objectives are cornerstones of the New Age movement which we shall look at in the next chapter. Our objective here is simply to note the political elements in the forces of change which are driving the world towards the point where international issues will be of such a magnitude that the demand for centralised authority will become irresistible and people will willingly submit to such an international authority, even surrendering their national and tribal freedoms in order to ensure survival. This does not mean that local and regional authorities will cease to exist but rather their powers will be curtailed in submission to the international authority.

We return to our question, Can we see the hand of God in all this? God has long ago declared his intention of bringing down unjust rulers and evil regimes. Mary rejoiced in the power of God to do just this when she visited her cousin Elizabeth before the birth of their sons who were to announce and inaugurate the reign of God. She sang:

> He has performed mighty deeds with his arm; he has scattered those who are proud in their inmost thoughts. He has brought down rulers from their thrones but has lifted up the humble (Lk 1:51–52).

We have already noted that God often simply awaits the wickedness of sinful regimes to run their course and sometimes he gives foreknowledge of this to his servants. God revealed to Jeremiah that the Babylonian Empire would last only seventy years (Jer 29:10).

It was exactly seventy years from the Bolshevik Revolution of 1916 when the beginning of the end of the Communist Empire of the Soviet Union and Eastern Europe occurred. Again, God gave forewarning of this to his servants and a number of prophecies were recorded that the USSR would not survive to the end of the century. At Easter 1986 there was a large international gathering in Jerusalem bringing together many Christians from different parts of the world having prophetic ministries. The clearest word to emerge at that time was that God was about to shake the nations and concurrently there would be a great harvest of the kingdom. Additionally, the word was spoken that the first nation to be shaken would be the Soviet Union. Three weeks later the world received the news of the melt-down at the Chernobyl nuclear power plant.

It was this event which triggered the sequence that led to the final dissolution of the USSR and the Soviet-led Communist Empire. A cloud of nuclear fallout descended upon the Ukraine, bread basket of the USSR, supplying up to one-third of the nation's grain. The land was rendered useless and President Gorbachev was forced to seek to buy grain from the USA. He could not do this without dollars. President Reagan agreed to help but at a price—the withdrawal of Soviet troops from Afghanistan. This brought a quarter of a million men back into the Soviet Union, many of whom were demobilised and had to be reabsorbed into the labour market. The creaking agricultural industry of the USSR had to be regalvanised to meet the emergency. This forced Gorbachev to institute a policy of reforms which could only be accomplished with the co-operation of the people. Hence reform and openness, *perestroika* and *glasnost* went hand-in-hand.

But the new freedom of expression given to the people resulted in demands for more, especially as the economic situation deteriorated and shortages of food and consumer goods became more acute. These demands became an irresistible clamour and gave rise to a tide of political protest which triggered the abortive right-wing backlash of 1989 which toppled Gorbachev. He was temporarily reinstated by the man who emerged as the hero of the hour, his arch rival Boris Yeltsin, who became President of Russia and leader of the newly emerging CIS at the beginning of 1990. The Communist Empire was dead. It had all begun with a comparatively small event, the accident in the nuclear power station at Chernobyl.

The significance of Chernobyl is often missed by political commentators. During World War Two it was the scene of a Jewish pogrom. The Ukrainians murdered an unknown number of Jews. They dug a mass grave and threw the bodies in. After the war they built the nuclear power plant directly on top of the mass Jewish grave. It was here that the melt-down took place—as though the blood of the innocent was crying out from the ground.

A further significant event had taken place three years earlier. In 1983 Chernobyl had been declared a model Communist commune. This meant, in effect, that only paid-up members of the Communist Party were allowed to live in the town and its surrounding area. In fact an area of thirty kilometres around Chernobyl was cleared of all non-Communist Party members. This forced the removal of those who were known to be Christians and Jews. The Christians were mainly Baptists and Pentecostals. This had the effect of taking from the area those who could intercede on behalf of the land. When the explosion occurred in April 1986 and nuclear radiation poured down upon the local population bringing slow death to thousands, the committed Christians and Jews had left the region. It is strange how the wickedness of men sometimes serves the purposes of God. As Joseph once said to his brothers, the things they meant for harm, God has worked out for good (Gen 50:20).

The forces of political change are blowing ever more strongly across the world. They have been generated in many respects by the evil policies of arrogant and oppressive rulers intent on building their own power bases and increasing their own personal wealth; but God has a way of humbling the mighty, of bringing down empires and of seeing to it that events knit together like the pieces of a jigsaw to accomplish his purposes. The God of history is active in the world, allowing the nations to exercise their own freedom of will but ensuring that the course of history will eventually reach his own predetermined goal. It is that goal that has been revealed to his servants and recorded in the Bible.

7

Family and Morality

The most striking indicator of national instability is not to be found in economic or political factors, or even in the crime statistics, but in the health of the family. The family is the core unit in every society. It is the most important social institution for maintaining stability in society. When family life is weakened every aspect of national life is affected. When the health of the family is impaired a whole variety of social diseases spreads through the nation. When the family breaks down, society breaks down.

The reason why the family is so essential to the health and stability of a nation is that it is from the family that we draw our identity and our security. The human baby is more helpless than any newborn in the animal world. It is completely dependent upon the adult humans around it for nurture and sustenance of life. Research has shown that what happens to us in the earliest years of life has a formative effect upon our personality and character development which in turn affects the whole of our life. If a child is brought up in a stable loving environment it is much more likely to develop a stable personality than a child reared in a turbulent environment.

The family not only feeds and clothes and protects the infant but also teaches him or her the standards of behaviour expected in society. Unlike animals, human beings are not born with strong instincts. Most of our behaviour is learned. This places an enormous responsibility upon those who are rearing children, not only to teach them the basics for survival, such as awareness of danger and how to communicate through language, but also the standards of right and wrong which are acceptable in society and which engender personal health as well as the public good. When the family is weak, child-rearing practices are neglected with severe consequences to both private and public morality.

There have been far-reaching and fundamental changes in the structure of the family and the function of family life throughout the world in the twentieth century. A wide range of factors have been responsible for this, such as the introduction of family planning, the widespread use of abortion, the changing social role of women, migration, the internal movement of population due to the growth of industry and the extensive growth of cities, the fragmentation of rural communities and weakening of village life, plus the changing perceptions of morality. The latter have been widely influenced by the growth of the film, television and video industries, especially in the second half of the century.

The most radical effects of the changes to the family are to be seen in the western industrialised nations with their advanced technologies and multi-media dominated cultures. If we look at the facts of family life in Britain today we see a vivid picture of a nation being shaken to its foundations. Perhaps the most startling statistic is the fact that by 1993 one-third of all babies born in Britain were born out of wedlock. This proportion had been steadily rising since the 1960s which saw the beginnings of the post-war pop culture, dominated by youth, the rejection of traditional norms and the rise of sexual promiscuity. This figure compares with fifty per cent in Denmark and Sweden, thirty per cent in France and twenty-six per cent in the USA.

The following table shows comparative figures until 1991. In all these western nations only Sweden had a birthrate outside of marriage in excess of ten per cent in 1960. This gives some measure of the rate of change in the breakdown of traditional family life in the western nations over a thirty-year period.

Live births outside marriage as a percentage of all births

Country	1960	1991
United Kingdom	5.0	30.0
Denmark	8.0	47.0
Sweden	11.0	49.0
France	6.0	26.0
Germany	8.0	15.0
USA	3.0	26.0

Source: Central Statistical Office
UK Government

The changes we are noting in the family have taken place in a single generation. This incredible speed is in itself a major factor in destabilising a society.

Of all the babies born out of wedlock in the UK seventy-five per cent are registered by both parents and half are registered by parents living at the same address. This provides some evidence that many of these babies may be born to parents living in stable relationships. There is, however, statistical evidence to show that those living in common law or unmarried relationships are more likely to split up than married couples. There is further statistical evidence showing that those who co-habit before marriage are more likely to divorce than those who come fresh into a marriage relationship.

Alistair Burt, a junior minister at the Home Office, referred to these facts (13th September 1994) when speaking about the problems of child care in the nation. He was criticised by the media for advocating 'traditional' values of the family, no doubt because he is known to be a committed Christian. The media in Britain have done much to undermine family values and, since the 1960s, have constantly pushed the boundaries of morality, particularly relating to sexual mores, further and further from traditional norms. Sexual promiscuity, adultery, unfaithfulness, homosexual practice, lying, cheating, deceiving and all kinds of deviant behaviour are regularly shown in the media in soaps, serials, family comedies and dramas. These have a formative effect upon the moral values of the nation, especially children and young people growing up in unstable home environments with the lack of teaching on firm basic principles of morality.

The effects of this lack of moral teaching upon the young are clearly shown in the sexual behaviour of girls in Britain. Eighty-three per cent of all babies born to teenage mothers in 1991 were outside marriage. In fact, the younger the mother, the more likely she is to be unmarried, and thirty-four per cent of all teenage conceptions in 1991 were terminated by abortion. Britain has the highest proportion of teenage pregnancies in Europe. This is said by many social workers to be attributable to inadequacies in sex education in schools. On the other hand, it may be argued that if the family was carrying out its traditional task of child-rearing effectively there would be no need for schools to do more than teach the biological facts. It should not be left to teachers to instruct children in basic morality or family values.

A further factor in the high rate of teenage conception outside wedlock and the large number of unmarried young people living together, is that in the economic climate of the 1990s with high rates of unemployment and a lack of job security among many of those who are in employment, has created a situation of social instability. Young men with few or no employment prospects do not make attractive husbands for girls looking for stability and security for themselves and their offspring. Many young girls, however, long to get away from home where parents fight and there is an unhappy atmosphere. They themselves are in search of emotional support, but rather than trust themselves to an uncertain partner they try living together for a period to see if it will work. Sadly, for many it does not work.

Single parents are the most rapidly expanding social group in modern Britain. In 1971 eight per cent of all families in the UK were led by a single parent; by 1991 this had more than doubled to eighteen percent. These figures include families of all types with dependent children. A truer picture of the state of family life in Britain is given by the numbers of single parents rather than these percentages. In 1991 there were 1,300,000 single parents caring for 2,100,000 children at a cost to the British taxpayer of £3.5b. It was in the light of this huge economic burden upon the nation that the government set up the Child Support Agency to try to track down errant fathers who were failing to give financial support to their children. The Agency, however, proved to be highly unpopular and dubious in its methods which created more problems than it solved.

The number of lone parents receiving Income Support from the State almost trebled in twelve years, from 395,000 in 1979 to 895,000 in 1991. During that same period the proportion of mothers receiving maintenance from the fathers of their children fell from fifty per cent to twenty-three per cent. By 1994 this had further fallen to twenty per cent. Thus eight out of ten lone parents were receiving no maintenance at all and were therefore either dependent upon their own earnings or dependent upon the State for housing, feeding and clothing their children. These figures not only are indications of sexual promiscuity, but they give a vivid picture of the fickleness, irresponsibility and lack of commitment to personal relationships of a large proportion of the population in Britain today.

This, in fact, is a reflection of attitudes to personal and public morality running right through the western nations. It is now the exception rather than the norm to make lifetime commitments as the figures for marriage and divorce illustrate. Since 1970 the trends have been divorce up, marriage down. Since 1971, when the Divorce Reform Act came into force, marriages have fallen by a fifth while divorces have doubled. There was a further noticeable rise in the number of divorces between 1984 and 1985 following the introduction of the Matrimonial and Family Proceedings Act which reduced the minimum period after marriage that a divorce petition could be filed. The comparative figures for divorce are:

1966	32,000
1971	110,000
1991	220,000

The average marriage in Britain today lasts only nine years and, perhaps even more significantly, one in ten marriages breaks down in under two years. This is a further factor showing a lack of commitment to building lasting personal relationships.

The increasing rate of breakdown in family life has brought suffering, not only to married couples and adult members of their families, but also untold suffering in the lives of children. Many of these children at a young age suffer the traumas of divided loyalties; of having to spend time first with one parent and then the other; of having to adjust to the acceptance of stepmothers or stepfathers and the inclusion of their children into the family circle.

With the current weaknesses in the family it is small wonder that we have been seeing a steady rise in juvenile crime in Britain for the past three decades. The nation has been shocked by some horrifying crimes of violence committed by quite young children. The murder in 1992 of the two-year-old James Bulger by two eleven-year-old boys stunned the nation. This was an act of premeditated slow torture and battering to death of a tiny helpless child whom they had abducted from his mother in a shopping mall. There was evidence that these children had seen a considerable number of explicitly violent videos and that they were probably acting out scenes which they had seen on the small screen. It was in the wake of the shock waves running through the nation following the James Bulger murder that the government introduced its ill-fated 'Back to Basics' campaign which was derided by the media and rendered untenable by the moral scandals in the lives of government ministers.

Further clear evidence of the plight of family life in Britain was provided by the numbers of children taken into care as being beyond parental control and the number of expulsions from school—66,000 in 1992. These figures, showing the behavioural problems of large numbers of children, are indicators of serious problems within the family life of the nation. The freedom from traditional constraints within the family, which were derided in the 1960s, have given way to an age not of joyful freedom, but of misery and despair for millions of children and young adults, many of whom are to be found homeless in the streets of British cities, begging by day and sleeping rough by night. Clearly there is something fundamentally wrong when a rich industrial nation with hundreds of years of social tradition and stability behind it suddenly, in a single generation, overturns all its basic norms and goes into a period of moral free-fall.

The situation in Britain is fairly typical of that which exists throughout the western nations. Yet strangely enough, although family life is disintegrating, the ideal of the family is actually rising in popularity. A European survey has shown that in the twelve nations of the European Union there is a significant difference between attitudes in 1981 and 1990. The question put to a representative sample in all these nations was, 'Does a child need both a father and a mother for its health, stability and happiness?' In 1981 the percentage responding positively was eighty-one but in 1990 this had risen to eighty-seven per cent. Thus the longing for the ideal of a stable family life is rising while, at the same time, the reality is declining. This, perhaps, is one of the few statistics on family life which gives a ray of hope for the future.

What is this ideal of family life for which there is a clear longing in the western nations today? And what has happened to the family in the twentieth century? What is it that has been lost in so short a period of history? The ideal is to be found in the biblical concept of the family, and it was this concept which was typical of family life throughout the western nations, with their centuries-old Christian tradition and teaching, at the beginning of the twentieth century.

In 1900 the predominant type of family in Britain could be described as a multi-generational unit, usually three generations, consisting of grandparents, parents and children plus aunts, uncles and cousins, all recognising common bonds of kinship. Usually all the members of the extended family would be living in a fairly close geographical location either in a rural village or in an urban setting. Often members of the same family would be engaged in the same kind of occupation, thus further reinforcing family solidarity. The family would give support to one another, especially in hard times or on special occasions such as weddings, birth and death.

By the middle of the century the predominant type of family had become the nuclear family consisting of mother, father and children economically independent from the rest of the family and usually living in geographical isolation.

By the final decade of the century the pattern of family life had changed yet again through increased mobility and the drift towards greater individualism in society so that the predominant type of family is now either two individuals co-habiting in shared accommodation with their children or a lone parent struggling to care for children in isolation from any kin group. Thus in a single century a radical shift has occurred from the extended family to the nuclear family to the one-parent family.

By contrast, the biblical model of the family is that of a multi-generational unit. This is linked to a clan, which is linked to a tribe, which in turn is linked to the nation. This is the concept of the family which we find in ancient Israel throughout the biblical period. This type of family structure produced a considerable level of both tribal and national solidarity. This was essential for national security and to guard against invasion from hostile forces. It was the family structure of Israel which created ties of loyalty of such strength that the whole tribe could be rapidly mobilised to defend its territory. If the threat was greater and more general the common origins of the tribes were invoked, calling upon them to act together in defence of one another.

In the Old Testament there are many examples of this tribal and national loyalty. A good example of the way the family structure of the nation engendered social solidarity and national loyalty can be seen in the account in Judges chapter 6 of the leadership exercised by Gideon when the territory of northern Israel was invaded by Midianites, Amalekites and other eastern peoples.

Once Gideon had experienced the call of God upon his life he tore down the family altar to Baal and cut down his father's Asherah pole. His father was evidently the head-man of the clan who all lived in the same location and were used to worshipping at the same altar. They quickly gathered to punish Gideon for his 'sacrilege' but Gideon's father restrained them saying that it was Baal who had been insulted so let him do his own punishing. When nothing happened to Gideon it was assumed that the God whom Gideon claimed to be serving was more powerful than Baal. Gideon, having gained the support of his own family and of the clan, the Abiezrites, used them as messengers to go throughout his tribe of Manasseh and into the neighbouring tribes of Asher, Zebulun and Naphtali (Judg 6:35).

The strength of inter-tribal loyalty can be measured by the fact that 32,000 men from the four tribes responded to Gideon's summons. Once the Midianites had been routed the tribe of Ephraim was also summoned to come down out of the hills and chase the enemy across the Jordan, thus clearing the entire area of north-eastern Israel. The strength of national solidarity was such that the Ephraimites grumbled to Gideon that he had not summoned them earlier to mobilise for the battle together with their brothers in the other tribes and it took all Gideon's diplomacy to calm their resentment.

A major function of the family in Israel was to provide the individual with an identity. In fact the closeness of family ties and responsibilities was such that no individual would be left in isolation. The whole concept of the individual separated from the family unit is foreign to biblical precepts.

Individualism is a modern western phenomenon which is essentially selfish and destructive of family life, which ironically in turn destroys individual lives. Throughout the Bible individuals are known by their family name and identified by their kinship group. Thus we find Saul son of Kish, or Jonathan son of Saul. The tradition of using family names was still strong in New Testament times, although in the Gospels, primarily written for mixed Jew and Gentile congregations, the kinship identities are not so significant. In the Gospels they are used to identify those of similar names from each other; for example, in the list of the twelve apostles in Matthew 10:2 James son of Zebedee is distinguished from James son of Alphaeus. On occasions Jesus used the full name probably by way of emphasis, as he did following Peter's acknowledgement of him as the Christ at Caesarea Philippi. 'Jesus replied, "Blessed are you, Simon son of Jonah"' (Mt 16:17).

Family ties were still very important within Israel at the time of Jesus. Jesus himself was known as the son of Joseph and both Matthew and Luke give extensive genealogies, Matthew tracing his family line back to Abraham which was of significance to the Jews to whom Matthew addressed his Gospel; and Luke, writing primarily for Gentiles, traced the genealogy right back to Adam.

The importance of the family and kinship structure in Israel is well illustrated in the account of Saul becoming king and establishing his place in the nation. The basic family unit was of three generations headed by the grandfather, hence we find Saul son of Kish son of Abiel. This family, according to 1 Samuel 10:21, was related to the clan of Matri who were part of the tribe of Benjamin in the nation of Israel. After the prophet Samuel had declared Saul to be king and presented him to the heads of the tribes he could not automatically command the respect of the whole nation, but when the town of Jabesh Gilead was attacked by the Ammonites who threatened to gouge out the right eye of every citizen, 'and so bring disgrace on all Israel' (1 Sam 11:2) this presented Saul with the opportunity of enforcing national solidarity. 'He took a pair of oxen, cut them into pieces, and sent the pieces by messenger throughout Israel, proclaiming "This is what will be done to the oxen of anyone who does not follow Saul and Samuel." Then the terror of the Lord fell on the people, and they turned out as one man' (v 7).

In the western nations today few people know anything of their family heritage beyond their own grandparents whom they have known personally. It is rare to find anyone who knows much about their grandfather's parents or could describe where they lived, what was their occupation or lifestyle. Yet in Israel this would have presented no difficulty. Of course, mobility was not a problem since territory remained within the clan very largely as it had been assigned at the time of the settlement in Canaan under Joshua's leadership. Anyone in Israel could tell you about their family and kinship group for many generations back and careful records of these were kept.

The first eight chapters of 1 Chronicles are an extensive list of the clans within the different tribes of Israel. The fact that these are recorded there underlines their importance in the life of the nation. Each of the tribes traced its line of descent back to one of the sons of Jacob (Israel). It was the bonds created by this common identity which gave character to the nation. The members of all the tribes were able to recognise each other as brothers due to their common ancestry and heritage. This was reinforced by the covenant made with Abraham and later confirmed and made more explicit through the ministry of Moses.

Every family and clan shared in the benefits and obligations of the covenant relationship with God which was part of the common heritage of the tribes. Thus, in a very real sense, the whole nation was conceived as being one family under God and God himself could refer to them as his children. When they were rebellious God had every right to complain, 'I reared children and brought them up, but they rebelled against me. The ox knows his master, the donkey his owner's manger, but Israel does not know, my people do not understand' (Is 1:2–3).

The strength of the message of the prophets was always based upon this special relationship between Israel and God. The prophets saw God sorrowing over his errant family, 'When Israel was a child I loved him, and out of Egypt I called my son. But the more I called Israel, the further they went from me . . . They did not realise it was I who healed them. I led them with cords of human kindness, with ties of love . . . ' (Hos 11:1–4).

This family-centred concept of society with Christ as the head is the ideal of the church presented in the New Testament. 'He is the head of the body, the church,' wrote Paul (Col 1:18). 'Now you are the body of Christ, and each one of you is a part of it' (1 Cor 12:27).

The apostles, with their Hebrew background and strong family ties, carried this understanding of family and nation over into the church. Paul saw this as part of the mystery of the gospel which had been hidden for ages but had now 'been revealed by the Spirit to God's holy apostles and prophets. This mystery is that, through the gospel, the Gentiles are heirs together with Israel, members together of one body and sharers together in the promise in Christ Jesus' (Eph 3:5–6). Thus the new kin-ship arrangement through Christ, who had broken down the barrier of hostility between Jew and Gentile, meant that God had actually created a new family structure bringing together people of all nations under the headship of Christ.

Peter perceived the transforming effect that acceptance of the gospel had upon people from different backgrounds, languages, cultures, and nations. He wrote of the church, 'You are a chosen people, a royal priesthood, a holy nation, a people belonging to God . . . Once you were not a people, but now you are the people of God' (1 Pet 2:9–10).

This was not a difficult concept for the believers in the apostolic church to grasp since it was not only Israel who recognised close family ties, the whole Roman Empire was built on a 'household' system in which the male head exercised a patriarchal authority over the clan. This was a very similar social structure to that of Israel, and indeed the whole Roman Empire was conceived since the time of the first Caesar as being one large household under the patrial authority of the emperor.

The family, both in ancient Israel and in the New Testament church, provided not only identity and security but also support and welfare for every member. The weak and the vulnerable were those whose natural family ties had been broken. Hence, in the New Testament, in the earliest days of the church, we find the apostles ensuring that widows and orphans were supported. Acts 6:1 refers to a daily distribution of food among the Hellenistic and Hebraic Jews. This was carrying over into the church the principle of caring for the most vulnerable members of the family that had always been the practice in Israel.

When Naomi was widowed, and her sons, who would normally have taken responsibility for caring for her, also died, she decided to go back to her clan territory. There she knew she would be cared for and find security. The beautiful story of Ruth accompanying her mother-in-law is an Old Testament classic, but it illustrates the strength of the family and its obligations and benefits as a model which promotes not only the security and wellbeing of the individual, but also the health of the whole nation. Naomi's kinsman, Boaz, gladly undertook his responsibilities for Ruth and Naomi including the care of the land that was theirs by right but for which a redemption price had to be paid. Although not the nearest kinsman he followed all the rules, and in the presence of the elders, the family, kinship responsibilities, rights and obligations, were transferred to him.

The story of Ruth and Boaz, who were ancestors of our Lord, comes to us in stark contrast to the weakness of the family and the plight of individuals in modern western society. Ruth's care for her mother-in-law was an obligation of love rather than the responsibility of kinship which makes the account all the more appealing, but in modern Britain the care of the elderly within the family is becoming increasingly rare. The combined effects of individualism and state welfare provision have weakened the obligations of the family, not only towards the elderly, but also towards the handicapped and children born with disabilities.

In Europe, with its ageing population and decreasing birthrate, this is a serious problem presenting the nations with immense economic burdens. Medical science is keeping the elderly alive longer and technological changes are reducing employment opportunities which combine to make a situation where fewer workers are having to support increasing numbers of dependants. Such a situation places an intolerable strain upon the economy. It is in the context of this situation that the subject of euthanasia is being discussed in the 1990s and creating genuine fears among the elderly and the disabled.

The economic burden upon the nations is increased by the number of one-parent families claiming welfare support and girls with babies requiring housing provision and with no other means of support.

Thus the loosening of family ties is creating an immense economic problem in nations where material wealth and economic prosperity are of paramount importance. The Capitalist system seeks to maximise profitability and minimise costs. Thus the social system is at variance with economic philosophy. When the point is reached when the burden becomes too great and the economic health and viability of the nation are threatened, welfare provision will be cut. The government has for a number of years been giving warnings that this might happen, and a variety of measures have been introduced to increase payments for medical services, cut down the payment of excessive benefits and expose fraudsters.

All these measures are seen as disastrous by people who have grown up in a welfare state used to relying on the provision of support from the cradle to the grave. Yet there is a sense in which this support has done immeasurable harm in removing basic responsibilities from the family and creating dependency upon the state. That is not to say that support for the weaker members of society such as widows and orphans should not be available, particularly for those in smaller or virtually non-existent family units. But if this support could be channelled through larger family and kinship groups it could be an important means of restoring the health of society by strengthening family ties.

At the same time as policies to strengthen the family are introduced, it is also necessary to tackle the causes of family breakdown. Undoubtedly one of these causes is the free availability of pornography both in magazines and on video film. There is a considerable body of evidence now linking pornography with domestic violence and the sexual abuse of both women and children. When men watch the sexual acrobatics and perversions shown in these video films, and their wives are unable to perform similar feats, it leads to dissatisfaction in the marriage bed and often to violence. This has become a major cause of marriage breakdown and the termination of common-law or co-habiting relationships. In today's permissive society there is no social stigma attached to breaking these relationships or to obtaining a divorce and seeking a new partner. A BBC *Newsnight* report in January 1994 estimated that by the age of fifty the average man in Britain has had thirteen different sexual partners.

In such a permissive social climate it is difficult to see how any form of stable family life can be created and maintained. It is therefore essential to tackle causes as well as to create new social policies which change attitudes and strengthen family life. As part of such policies, curbing the free availability of pornography must surely be essential. On the positive side it is equally essential to promote the kind of family structure which will give much needed identity, support and security to the individual. Such a family structure will also give basic teaching in morality which, within a generation or two, could totally transform the whole social situation in the nation. The biblical model of the family is the God-given means of promoting the true health and welfare of the nation.

One of the major weaknesses in launching a Christian campaign to promote the biblical ideal of family life lies within the church itself where, among many clergy and lay leaders, there is a lack of strong biblical convictions. The year 1994 was supposed to be the international year of the family but very little was heard of creative new policies on family life. The major international event, held in September of that year, was an international conference on population control in Cairo. The focus there was on how to prevent more babies being born in the poorer nations rather than how to promote and strengthen healthy family life in all nations.

In Britain too often church reports on family and matters relating to morality have been influenced by liberal theologians who have all too scant regard for biblical standards. Thus the church has given an uncertain sound on fundamental issues such as homosexuality, divorce, faithful marriage relationships, family responsibilities for the young, the vulnerable and the elderly.

The biblical model of the family has not been upheld before the nation as the ideal given by God for people of all nations, neither has it been practised by Christians, even those with strong biblical traditions. Marriage breakdown among Christians has become all too common in all branches of the church since the 1960s. This invasion of the church by the world, bringing with it its own standards of morality, is the exact reversal of the biblical pattern of evangelism established by Jesus in the Great Commission given to the apostles, 'Go and make disciples of all nations, baptising them in the name of the Father and of the Son and of the Holy Spirit, and teaching them to obey everything I have commanded you' (Mt 28:19).

The preaching of the gospel includes making disciples for the Lord Jesus and teaching them to obey his commandments. These include the indissolubility of marriage and of faithful obligations within the family. Jesus' command to his disciples that we should love one another means revolutionary changes in personal relationships and the establishment of standards which are quite different from those of the world.

By losing its concept of the God of history who is

working out his good purposes in the world, the church has lost its power to influence the nations for good. With the recovery of that understanding, basic to the biblical revelation of God, will come the recovery of the power to declare the word of God with authority among the nations. God has given us the right pattern for the family which promotes the health and happiness of each individual. It is when we go against this and try to reorder society according to our own evil desires that misery and suffering are created and the exploitation and abuse of the weak and the vulnerable occur. Strong family ties and a family-centred society are the proper ordering for the nation and these protect the individual from such exploitation and enable each individual the freedom to develop their own gifting within a supportive structure.

The God of history is allowing the rebellion of mankind to run its full course as he did in Israel when he allowed the Babylonians to overrun the land and to destroy Jerusalem, taking tens of thousands into captivity. It was the experience of suffering through seventy years of exile that brought the nation to its senses and created the conditions for repentance and crying out to God for forgiveness that led to restoration. God worked out his purposes for Israel by breaking the power of Babylon and restoring the people to the land. They immediately set about restoring the family life of the nation as is recorded in Nehemiah and the genealogy in 1 Chronicles 3:17–24. Clearly they saw the re-establishment of family life and responsibilities as being essential to the recovery of the nation.

This is the message which the church should be proclaiming in these days of family breakdown. God is allowing the sinfulness of man to reach the point where we recognise the misery and suffering that our own wickedness, individualism and self-centredness have brought upon us. Now is the time for the church to call for repentance and to cry out to God for forgiveness, that the time of restoration may be hastened. The proclamation of such a message will only come from a church that recognises the activity of God in history and acknowledges the way in which he is longing to work out his good purposes in the world today. It is also essential that the church acknowledges and declares publicly the provision God has made for the forgiveness of sins through the Lord Jesus Christ and the renewal of the national way of life through the restoration of right relationships within the family as the core unit of society.

8

Spiritual Forces of Change

The twentieth century has seen astonishing changes in the religious scene throughout the world. During the first half of the century religion appeared to be on the decline, while the second half of the century has seen a phenomenal growth in its significance, particularly in the last quarter of the century in the run-up to the end of the millennium.

Two world wars in the first half of the century added to the general disillusionment and questioning of traditional values which had been growing in momentum since the eighteenth-century Enlightenment. The western world was in the forefront of this process of intellectual and spiritual nihilism. Church attendance in Europe declined steadily, although in America it held fairly constant. The rise of Communism and the increasing secularism throughout the western world led many to believe, by the middle of the century, that religion was a thing of the past.

Religion played very little part in the movement towards independence from European colonialism in Africa and Asia. A notable exception was the religious tensions in India at the time of Independence in 1947 which led to the partition between the Muslim north and the Hindu, Sikh and Christian populations of central and

126

southern India. This led to the formation of Pakistan, eventually to become an Islamic state.

It was not until the 1960s that a worldwide revival in religion began to appear. The triumph of Communism, one of whose objectives was the eradication of religion, appeared to be complete; yet there were many reports that Christianity was far from dead in the Soviet Union or in eastern European nations such as Poland which were under the control of the USSR. News of internal affairs in China was more difficult to obtain but at the time of the 1949 Communist triumph there were said to be fewer than one million Christians in the whole of China and this was following 100 years of western missionary endeavour. Yet by 1980, following the death of Mao Tse Tung and the opening up of communications with the West, it was discovered that Christianity had become indigenised and had grown to a potent underground force throughout the years of severe persecution under the Maoist Communist regime. At that time it was estimated that there were at least fifty million Christians in China, mostly in the underground churches. By 1990 that figure was reliably estimated to have at least doubled to 100 million, still mainly in the underground, that is, the unregistered, churches.

South Korea, recovering from the ravages of the north/south war of the 1950s, was another place where Christianity began to expand rapidly in the burgeoning western-type post-war economy. The number of Christians in South Korea in 1955 was said to be less than five per cent, by 1975 the proportion had risen to sixteen per cent and by 1990 it had reached nearly thirty per cent.

The second half of the twentieth century has seen religion increasingly become an area of social and international conflict. The separation of India and Pakistan in 1947 resulted in severe Muslim/Hindu rioting causing several million deaths, including the assassination of

Mahatma Gandhi in 1948. It is a conflict which has rumbled on ever since with apparently no end in sight. Religious conflict in India has been further exacerbated by Sikh extremism, which resulted in the assassination of Prime Minister Indira Gandhi after troops assaulted the Sikh's Golden Temple in Amritsar in 1984.

The most significant escalation of religious conflict in the second half of the century has been the rise of militant Islamic fundamentalism. When the Shah of Iran was forced into exile in January 1979, Ayatollah Khomeini, who had been in exile since 1963, returned to Teheran in triumph and formed an Islamic revolutionary council to govern the country and transform it into the most militant religious state in the modern world. Numerous terrorist atrocities have been linked to Iran or thought to have been initiated from there. Many other religious conflicts have occurred in the last quarter of the twentieth century particularly involving Islamic fundamentalists. These have been especially bitter in Israel where the political struggle with the PLO has been complicated by Muslim extremists such as Hamas. Additionally, there have been bitter conflicts between Muslims and Christians in Ethiopia, Sudan, Chad and Nigeria. The rise of fundamentalist Islam as an aggressive international force has been a major characteristic of the last quarter of the twentieth century.

It is always of interest to note the socio/cultural roots of any new religious movement. Islamic fundamentalism arose out of the centuries-old hostility between Sunni and Shi'ite groups within the Muslim faith, which culminated in the eight-year war between Iraq and Iran in the 1980s. The Shi'ites had always seen themselves as the poor relations of the Sunnis and had been looking for an opportunity to assert themselves. The formation of the State of Israel in 1948 was seen throughout the Islamic

world as an offence against Allah and this was the underlying reason for the Arab/Israeli wars and the years of
conflict that have followed. Iranian Shi'ites from their
bases in Lebanon have continued to be a sore in the side
of Israel for decades. One of Ayatollah Khomeini's major
objectives was the retaking of Jerusalem and this has
remained an important objective of Islamic fundamentalism. If he had succeeded in this it would have been a
tremendous boost to Shi'ite morale and a notable victory
in their desire to assert themselves over the Sunnis.

In the rich industrial nations of the West, Christianity
has not only been the dominant religion for centuries but
has also been largely responsible for forming the culture,
the basis of morality, the legal and the social structure.
The decline in church attendance throughout Europe has
continued right through the century and has had important
repercussions in every aspect of life. Notably, as the
churches have lost their power to influence the nations,
a spiritual vacuum has been left behind which, during the
second half of the century, has been filled by a wide
variety of spiritual phenomena. These have ranged from
the New Age movement to the exuberance of the charismatic movement, and from right-wing moral-majority
biblical fundamentalists to extreme liberal social-action
groups.

A spiritual vacuum never exists for long; as G. K.
Chesterton dryly observed, 'When men cease to believe
in God they do not believe in nothing, they believe in
anything!' That has certainly been the case in the post-
Christian industrialised western nations. The legacy of
nineteenth-century biblical Christianity lasted only one
generation into the twentieth century of decline in church
attendance. By the middle of the century that rich spiritual
heritage had run dry and as the new pop culture of the
1960s took a war-weary world by storm it provided just

the kind of fertile ground needed to spawn a wide variety of new religions.

In the decaffeinated world of California, cults of all kinds were born and flourished. Their bizarre beliefs, offering the elixir of eternal life, were matched only by their strange practices which made the holy-rollers of early Pentecostalism look like Orthodox priests. Some of these cults ended in tragedies which hit the world head-lines, such as the 900 followers of the Reverend Jim Jones who committed mass suicide in Guyana, and the fireball that consumed the followers of David Koresh at Waco, Texas in 1993. In Los Angeles alone there are said to be fifty different religious organisations, quite apart from the multitude of churches of different denominations.

In April 1995, two years to the day after the Waco seige, the city offices in Oklahoma were bombed, with devastating results. A car bomb left in an underground car park completely wrecked the building, causing more than 160 deaths, including many children in a day nursery. This act of terrorism was allegedly linked with an extreme right-wing militant pseudo-religious cult with millennial-ist beliefs. This sent shock waves throughout America, with forebodings of fear in the run-up to the year AD 2000.

In 1975 the New Age movement officially went public. Unlike the cults, New Age teaching offers an intellectual approach to humanity's quest for meaningful relationships with the supernatural and for fulfilling personal lifestyles. Helena Petrova Blavatsky, a nineteenth-century Russian emigrant to the USA, is generally accorded with being founder of the modern New Age movement. She predicted that her teaching would go underground for one hundred years, emerging in 1975 to form the basis for the new age which would soon dawn. Blavatsky's disciple, Alice Bailey, has been more influential in planning New Age strategy. Bailey claimed to receive her 'inspiration' from an eighth century Tibetan monk who channelled spiritual revelation to her. Her writings were published by the Lucifer Publishing Company which in 1922 became the Lucis Trust and is today the major organisation promoting New Age ideology, along with its action-arm 'World Goodwill'.

New Agers believe the world is on a 2000-year cycle linked with the signs of the zodiac and that the year 2000 will signal the beginning of the new age of Aquarius, the water-carrier. The New Age, symbolised by the water of life, will be an age of renewed spirituality which will bring about a basic change in the way humankind thinks and acts due to its new spiritual relationship to the cosmos. They believe it will be an age of new spiritual harmony breaking down the old order of mankind's exploitation of the physical world and bringing about a new harmony of mind and matter as men and women discover their true place in the created order. Through this harmony of humanity and creation new spiritual energies of creativity will be released into the world. These spiritual forces will transform relationships and initiate a new age of global peace and harmony in which individuals will achieve their true potential.

Hugely influential in New Age thinking have been the writings of Pierre Teilhard de Chardin, a Jesuit priest who died in 1955, whose essays *The Spiritual and Physical Evolution of the Universe* broke new ground in Christian mysticism. His ideas have been further developed by Matthew Fox, a current theological guru of the New Age movement. Fox was, until 1992, a Dominican priest but was dismissed from the order because of his theological views. He developed the concept of 'creation-centred spirituality' through which human beings can enter into a state of 'original blessing' by coming into harmony with mother nature and allowing the creative life from creation itself to flow through them, thus obviating the concept of sin and the need for a saviour.

The appeal of this type of thinking may be seen at St James, Piccadilly, in the fashionable West End of London, where Fox's theology and a range of New Age practices have been popularised by Donald Reeves since the mid-1980s. Reeves sees traditional biblical Christianity as failing to meet the needs of modern humanity and he has introduced a range of 'alternatives' based on multi-religious concepts, including many pagan, occult and eastern religious practices. Over the past decade there has been a steady growth in the number of clergy embracing New Age teachings and practices in Britain. In America the leading New Age church is the Cathedral of St John the Divine in New York City where David Spangler, one-time co-leader of the Findhorn Foundation in Scotland, is based. Spangler promotes the concepts of channelling energies and messages from spiritual powers, as well as ideas of reincarnation and personal transformation through which people can discover the reality of their inner self, the 'divine essence' within.

New Age concepts of spirituality are big business in the USA. Books on personal spiritual growth and related themes are regularly in the top ten non-fiction book lists. In August 1994 W. H. Smith in Britain announced its intention of following the American trend and installing a 'personal development' section in 500 of their bookshops throughout the UK. Reporting this, *The Times* said:

Without doubt there is a sudden international hankering for the spiritual and mystical. But why? There is no parallel return to organised religion. The trend is much more DIY, and the faith expected of readers is of an undemanding, semi-committed nature, without the effort required of mainstream church life. Nor do most of these books have a dark side;

Satan and the wages of sin tend to go unmentioned. Welcome to the saccharin universe of New Age theology.

In America the publishers Warner Books have their own theory accounting for the popularity of books on spirituality: 'It has a lot to do with an industrial society in which the one thing that seems to unify us these days is that there's a spiritual void in our lives.' In Britain the publishers Element Books believe the spiritual revival is linked with the approaching end of the millennium:

> If one looks at the end of any century it happens. Look at the huge religious revival at the end of the nineteenth century. Another catalyst might be the disillusionment at the end of the '80s with material life, and people saying, 'There must be something else.' (*The Times*, 16th August 1994.)

One hardly needs to be a prophet to predict a spiritual revival in the closing years of the twentieth century. It is not a question of whether or not there will be a revival but rather of what kind of revival it will be! The final years of any century have an unsettling effect upon the population; drawing to the close of a millennium has an even more traumatic effect. People are unsure of the future. A new millennium appears to be like entering another world. In our post-Christian western agnosticism most people lack the security of a firm faith to carry them through into an uncertain future.

The rapid growth of the charismatic movement since the mid-1960s is further evidence of the spiritual hunger of late-twentieth-century humanity. Although the charismatic movement has many similar spiritual characteristics to those of its Pentecostal counterpart there are some important differences in terms of its social history. The modern Pentecostal movement began in 1906 in a small back-street mission in Asuza Street, Los Angeles. Its immediate appeal was to black people and poor whites.

Although it grew considerably in the States during the first half of the century, in Britain its numbers were quite small and it never broke free from its working-class origins.

All that changed with the birth of the charismatic movement. Pentecostalism became respectable. The Four Square Gospel sect became a denomination and marked its new status with a change of name to become the Elim Pentecostal Church. People from all branches of the mainline churches—Catholics, Anglicans and free churches— began speaking in tongues and practising other spiritual gifts. But the charismatic movement did not have universal appeal at the start. In Britain it began in the 1960s, the decade of protest, of challenge to tradition, and the introduction of new standards of morality and behaviour. It began on the fringes of the church with house groups and small communities. By the end of the decade several Anglican clergy had received a new experience of the Holy Spirit, such as Michael Harper who formed the Fountain Trust, and Trevor Dearing at Hainault in Essex and Colin Urquhart at Luton, each of whom attracted considerable attention and ministered to packed congregations, which was all against the tide of decline in those days. Small communities of charismatics began to appear, such as Post Green near Bournemouth, with its connection with Canford Magna parish church and the ministry of John Collins who was later to move to Holy Trinity, Brompton in the fashionable heart of London's West End.

But the real breakthrough of the charismatic movement into the middle classes came with David Watson who, from his base in York, began touring the country with a team. They held meetings which were both evangelistic and offered a new kind of ministry bringing people into a fresh experience of the Holy Spirit, physical and spiritual healing and the personal experience of spiritual gifts. During the 1970s the renewal movement gathered momentum and by 1980 David Watson's ministry was impacting most of the mainline churches. The breakthrough into the middle classes was a watershed. Here was a man with a Cambridge background, who spoke in cultured tones of a new satisfying, personal relationship with God into which he himself had entered.

Billy Graham in the 1950s had made it socially acceptable for people of all classes to talk about religion; something the British had traditionally left to the clergy and the working classes—the Salvation Army, Church Army, Pentecostals, Welsh revivalists and Primitive Methodists. But this was something new. Here was the opportunity for ordinary people not simply to be offered salvation, but to be able to participate in the exercise of spiritual gifts.

The 1980s saw the charismatic movement develop in two significant directions. It penetrated all the mainline churches as a movement of spiritual renewal, transforming worship, creating more opportunities for personal participation for lay people, thus moving away from the dominance of the priest/minister syndrome which had professionalised ministry and shut lay people out from active participation in the church for hundreds of years. The second major development was the growth of the house churches into a new independent sector, first in rented buildings such as school halls and later owning their own buildings. Many of these new independent congregations grew at the expense of the traditional churches, although by the end of the 1980s most of them were outward-looking in terms of evangelism and social service, bringing a new atmosphere of confidence to evangelicalism in Britain.

The great economic recession of the early 1990s brought hardship and suffering to the British middle and upper classes for the first time since the 1920s. This had a spiritual impact of great significance which sent shock waves right through the country. As the economic prosperity of the 1980s evaporated and the rich had to tighten their belts and even sell their houses to meet their Lloyds Underwriters obligations, their confidence in the things they had traditionally taken for granted was shaken.

Despite the Conservatives being re-elected in 1992, the writing was on the wall for the British establishment rocked by one scandal after another hitting the rich, the powerful and even the Royal Family, so that even the monarchy itself appeared to have an uncertain future. The Tories had lost confidence in themselves and their own ability to solve the intractable economic problems, or to counter the ever-mounting tide of crime and violence, plus the evidence of social decay and family and moral breakdown sweeping the country. Those institutions, once thought to be founded upon rock, were seen to be built on sand. The whole British way of life was crumbling. The professionals and managerial classes were being forced into early retirement, made redundant or facing the fear of unemployment for the first time, or having to accept short-term contracts instead of lifetime security.

The spiritual impact of these revolutionary social and economic changes in the early 1990s began to have immediate effect in creating a spiritual hunger that had not been present in the British middle and upper classes since the First World War and its aftermath. Those days led to the Great Depression but the 1990s look set to lead to a Great Revival. Why the difference?

The new factor in the 1990s is the social acceptability of self-expression. The traditional British stiff upper lip has sagged under the impact of loss of Empire, world status, economic wealth and the succession of social changes which have descended like hammer blows upon traditional British mores. By the mid-1990s the evidence of personal stress was so widespread that to be 'with it' one could not be without it! It was the exception rather than the rule to be unruffled by the universal problems besetting the world and the apparent hopelessness of the human condition. Americans turned increasingly to their psychoanalysts while the British turned to their spiritual gurus—either from eastern religions or from southern California.

Thus the shaking of the nations has created a deep longing for spiritual security, for eternal values in an uncertain world. But the me-centred individualism of western culture, which has had a strong influence upon evangelical theology throughout the twentieth century, has had an even greater influence upon the teaching and practice of the charismatic movement.

In the early years of the renewal in Britain, those who broke away from the mainline churches in order to form independent fellowships were mostly those with little or no formal theological education. But the house-church leaders of the 1970s have become the apostles of the 1990s with vastly increased influence. Their emphasis is still upon what they call 'heart knowledge' rather than 'head knowledge'; in other words the elevation of experience over doctrine. The obvious danger of such an emphasis is that it moves away from biblical foundations. The rejection by evangelicals of liberal biblical scholarship has been a major factor in the loss of confidence in biblical scholarship per se. This has been instrumental in producing a version of Christianity lacking in strong biblical foundations, an Ishmael rather than an Isaac, one in which the Hebrew roots of the faith are given little emphasis in a welter of experiential excitement.

The effect of the social acceptability of personal self-expression was seen in 1994 in the ready and often uncritical welcome given to the so-called Toronto Blessing or 'laughing revival' by churches such as Holy

Trinity, Brompton with its upper-middle-class congregation. Many other middle-class congregations also embraced this new spiritual phenomenon which allowed people to give vent to their feelings by shouting, screaming or laughing hysterically, waving their arms or falling down.

For many of those who experienced the 'blessing' this was a new behavioural element which was described by their spiritual leaders as 'a time of refreshing' when God was allowing them to release the stress and pent-up tensions within them. They believed God was bringing them into a new relationship with himself in which they could experience a joyous release from problems of the world and experience his love and power in their lives.

Undoubtedly this has been true for many who were nominal believers or traditional evangelicals, as well as for those who were already charismatic. There are nevertheless serious dangers in an experientially based faith which leaves the believer swaying with every changing wind of spiritual fashion. There is an even greater danger as the popularity of experiential faith moves deeper into the mainline churches through the pressures to conform that are being experienced by leaders, ministers, pastors and elders. The growing churches are seen as the successful churches and these are the congregations where experiential faith is at its height and biblical teaching is often at a low ebb.

The great danger facing the church at this time is that it may miss its place in the purposes of God. The current lack of understanding of the God of history, the God who was known by his deeds throughout the times of biblical revelation, is actually placing in jeopardy the working out of the purposes of God at a crucial period in world history. It has always been God's intention to use his people of the New Covenant, those brought into a covenant relationship with himself through the blood of the Lord Jesus, to play a significant part in the new heavens and the new earth that he would in due time establish. Paul refers to this in Ephesians 3:10.

Many of the teachings of the new independent churches have spread right through the charismatic movement reinforcing the 'replacement theology' of the mainline churches which gives no place to Israel. They see the church as the inheritor of *all* the promises given to Israel whom she has totally replaced. Thus the modern state of Israel and the Jewish people play no further part within the purposes of God. These teachings overlook the fact that it was Israel who broke the covenant with God; nowhere in the New Testament is it even hinted that God has broken his covenant with Israel or ceased to love the people whom he called to be his servants despite their waywardness and rebellion.

It is often overlooked that the New Covenant described by Jeremiah in 31:31f would be made 'with the house of Israel and with the house of Judah'! It makes no mention of Gentiles being included. That same chapter ends with God's solemn declaration that he would never break his covenant of love with Israel throughout all generations. 'This is what the Lord says: "Only if the heavens above can be measured and the foundations of the earth below be searched out will I reject all the descendants of Israel because of all they have done"' (v 37). Paul certainly did not apply that promise to the Gentile church. He looked forward to the day when all Israel would be saved (Rom 11:26) and they (the Jews) would be 'grafted back into their *own* olive tree' (Rom 11:24).

To say that God has now finished with the descendants of Israel is to make God a liar. Moreover, if we cannot trust God to keep his own covenant with Israel how can we trust him to keep his covenant with us? Additionally, if we miss the significance of the regathering of the people of the Old Covenant into the land of Israel as prophesied by Jesus in Luke 21:24 in his reference to 'Jerusalem will be trampled on by the Gentiles until the time of the Gentiles are fulfilled', then we miss one of the major signs heralding his own Second Coming.

Jesus gave a number of indicators which would be signs of the nearness of his own return, one of which is of the gospel being preached 'in the whole world' (Mt 24:14). The phenomenal worldwide growth of the church throughout the second half of the twentieth century must surely be considered as a major sign of the times. This would be significant even if we did not take it in the context of all the other indicators which Jesus gave in Matthew 24, such as false christs, wars and rumours of wars, famines, earthquakes and persecution of believers, all of which are being seen today.

The church worldwide is growing, at the end of the twentieth century, at a faster rate than at any time since the first century when, under the impact of the ministry of the apostles, the gospel spread across the Roman world. The last two or three decades of the twentieth century have seen an explosion in the growth of the church in Asia, Africa and South America. It is significant that these are the poorer, less industrialised nations where the gospel is coming as good news to the poor, liberating those in bondage to pagan religions and bringing new life and hope to millions. In many of these countries believers are experiencing severe persecution from political authorities or religious fundamentalists, particularly those of Islam. But, as Tertullian observed, 'The blood of the martyrs is the seed of the church,' and the church continues to grow even under the most severe conditions.

In addition to the worldwide harvest of the gospel which is being seen today, it is surely significant that an ever-increasing number of Jewish people throughout the world, including in Israel, are becoming believers in Jesus. In fact David Barratt, in *The World Christian Encyclopedia*, records that, in proportion to their numbers, more Jews are accepting Jesus as Messiah than any other ethnic group in the world.

These Messianic believers now form a significant minority in Israel itself and are beginning to be heard despite the vehement opposition of the ultra-Orthodox. Messianic congregations, worshipping in Hebrew and openly declaring that they are believers in Jesus the Messiah of Israel, are a reminder that in the days immediately following Pentecost Jewish believers were the totality of the church. Throughout the first century they formed a significant part of the church and were not finally eradicated from the land until the brutal suppression of the Bar-Kochba revolt which began in AD 132. This was followed by a general expulsion of the Jews from the land of Israel which the Romans then renamed 'Palestine' as a deliberate insult to the Jews, with its insinuation of 'Philistine' occupation. They also renamed Jerusalem 'Aelia Capitalino'—but this never really caught on!

The Messianic fellowships today are bringing a new and exciting dimension into the worldwide church through their understanding of Hebrew customs and culture. Western theologians have long recognised the value of 'contextualisation', that is, seeing the Scriptures in the context of the times in which the different books of the Bible were written. This is bringing new understanding to our study of the words of the prophets of ancient Israel and is of especial value in understanding the life and times of Jesus and the apostolic church.

This study of the Hebrew roots of the faith has additional value in enabling us to recover an understanding of the God of history which was basic to the faith of Israel under the Old Covenant. From the eighth century onwards all the prophets exercised their ministries within the context of an understanding that God was not only active within Israel but in the affairs of the surrounding nations. The Bible thus reveals a God of purpose who, despite the freedom he has given to men and women, nevertheless steadily works out his purposes through the unfolding pages of history. Despite the sinfulness and rebelliousness of humanity God still touches the lives of those who will respond to his word and uses them to fulfil his purposes and to guide the destiny of the nations.

God's people of the Old Covenant are still loved by him and will never be rejected despite their own sinful ways and rejection of him. It is a sign of his mercy that he has brought them back into the land in a state of unbelief. But this is all part of his purposes as he is revealing himself to an increasing number of Jews. Messianic leaders in Israel testify that a large proportion of Jewish believers have not been evangelised by others but have come to faith through a direct revelation of Jesus. This may be a prophetic application of the story of Joseph who was rejected by his brothers because he claimed a special relationship with God and was sold into slavery in Egypt where he became great and powerful. God used him not only to save the Egyptians, but also to save Israel in a time of famine. In due time his own brothers went to him to buy corn and Joseph, having turned the Egyptians out of the room, revealed himself to his brothers and embraced them.

Jesus, having been rejected by his brothers, and having become greatly honoured among the Gentiles, is now revealing himself to his brothers.

9

Stabilising Values

Beliefs and values form the foundation of national life. They give identity and character to a nation. The people who belong to that nation recognise these characteristics when they meet up with their fellow countrymen in any part of the world. The values underlying a nation also give purpose and direction to national life. These are particularly important in times of crisis. Through a shared set of values the leaders of the nation are able to call upon the loyalty and service of all its citizens.

When war is declared the nation closes ranks, internal differences are set on one side, the beliefs and values of a nation are reaffirmed publicly and they reinforce national solidarity. During World War Two political party differences were shelved in Britain and a coalition government of national unity was formed. The church rallied behind the government and declared it to be a just war in which the nation was not simply fighting for personal survival but combating evil on behalf of all freedom-loving peoples. Thus, the values of loyalty, self-sacrifice, service, freedom and love for others were all emphasised. They were recognised as being part of the foundational values of the nation.

Today many commercial firms and industries regard values as of great importance for their efficient and effective operation in world markets. The Japanese have been pioneers in what is now recognised as a 'quality revolution' in industry which has taken the Japanese to a position of dominance in the world economy. Basic to this quality revolution has been the recognition that management processes are the key to efficiency. This principle has been developed by Stephen Covey who has described the concept of 'principle-centred leadership'. He argues that the designers of industrial processes incorporate their values into them. It is therefore essential to understand the values as well as the mission of an organisation in order to improve all aspects of its performance (Stephen Covey, *The Seven Habits of Highly Effective People* [New York: Simon and Schuster, 1989]).

In recent years 'quality awards' have been devised for industrial and commercial efficiency in a number of western industrialised nations. These awards require evidence of the implementation of 'vision', 'mission' and 'values'. This is using language remarkably similar to that which has been used in the church for many decades. Its significance is the recognition in secular society that it is values rather than material possessions which ultimately determine the success of institutions which depend upon human relationships and interaction for their effective functioning. If this is true for an industry or for a commercial enterprise, it is undoubtedly true for a community or a nation. Without a clear set of values, or principles, there can be no clear vision, and without vision there can be no clear sense of direction, or mission. When a nation's values are undermined that whole nation is set dangerously adrift.

The shaking of the nations which has been gathering momentum throughout the twentieth century has had a far-reaching effect upon most nations in the world. Revolutionary social changes have disturbed the foundational value system underlying many nations, thus intensifying the impact of social change and creating conditions of instability and uncertainty. There are numerous examples in the modern world of this happening.

The history of China during the second half of the twentieth century presents a fascinating story for social historians. In 1949 the successful Communist revolution led by Mao Tse Tung destroyed the Ming dynasty which had ruled China for many hundreds of years. In fact the political changes destroyed the social characteristics of a nation which had lasted for thousands of years. Then in 1965 the cultural revolution took place which aimed, not at the social structure which had already been effectively revolutionised, but at the value system underlying the nation. The aim was to destroy religion and to change the basic belief system which was linked with Buddhism and ancestor worship. These beliefs and values had given stability to the social structure of China for thousands of years. Once they were destroyed the door was open for the new social order to proceed without opposition.

There was, however, a strange by-product which China's atheist leaders could not have foreseen. In destroying the traditional beliefs and values of the nation they believed they were paving the way for the establishment of Marxist values. But what happened was the creation of a spiritual vacuum which paved the way for the rapid expansion of Christian evangelism such as we are seeing in China today. Buddhism and ancestor worship had been the chief barriers to the gospel throughout a hundred years of western Christian missionary enterprise. In 1949, when the Communists took over China, they closed the churches, publicly burned Bibles, expelled western missionaries and imprisoned Chinese pastors. It appeared to be the end of Christianity in that nation. But, as we have seen, in 1949 there were fewer than one million committed

Christians in the whole of China, whereas by 1990 it was estimated there were at least 100 million believers and that number was growing rapidly, probably at the rate of 25,000 new believers a day!

Unwittingly the Communist rulers of China prepared the way for the greatest explosion of the church in any nation in modern history. When Mao Tse Tung died in 1977 and the authorities began releasing imprisoned Chinese Christians in 1979 they unloosed into China a small but unstoppable spiritual force—Christians who had been purged in the fires of persecution and whose faith had come through untarnished and strengthened beyond any power to break. Their witness as they moved across China brought a message of salvation and hope to a hungry people enchained in the spiritual vacuum of a drab Communist existence. The good news was received with great joy and spread like wildfire as each one testified to his neighbour or brother or sister and the gospel spread from village to village and town to town. With the values and belief systems of the old order gone the nation was ripe for the new beliefs and values which the gospel provides.

The situation created in the CIS following the rapid demise of the Soviet Union is another example of the social effects of disturbing the value system underlying a nation. We have seen how, in April 1986, when the Chernobyl nuclear power plant exploded, it set off a chain reaction across the USSR. The resulting food shortages necessitated buying grain on the world market which required international currency of which the Soviets were short. They were forced to introduce the policies of *glasnost* and *perestroika*, the twin programmes of openness and reform. These were necessary in order to try and enlist the support of the population in cranking up the highly inefficient agricultural system and the creaking industrial economy.

But policies designed to increase the people's awareness of national needs and to enlist greater co-operation, paved the way for the undermining of the entire value system which had undergirded the totalitarian Communist state for seventy years. Critics of the system were quick to seize the opportunity of exercising their new freedom of expression and the ill-fated hard line attempted coup of 1989 accelerated the final demise of the USSR.

This rapid change in the political structure affected the whole social order and undermined the value system which threw the door wide open to anarchy. Crime rates soared, a black market flourished in the context of a shortage of food and consumer goods and of soaring inflation with unstable currency. This in turn encouraged the development of the Russian mafia and large-scale crime syndicates selling anything to the highest bidder on the international market, including sophisticated weapons and nuclear materials. This contrast between the tight controls exercised by a centrally organised government and the conditions of lawlessness which followed the collapse of the USSR primarily stemmed from the undermining of the value system.

Many other examples could be given, such as the war in the former Yugoslavia involving Croats, Bosnian Muslims and Serbs. Old inter-tribal enmities going back decades suddenly surfaced with the breakdown of the political structure. Moral precepts were swept aside in an orgy of bloodletting, rape and pillage. The values which had allowed Muslim, Orthodox and Catholic to live alongside one another as neighbours suddenly gave way to the principle of ethnic cleansing. Tribal madness suddenly replaced the values of humanitarian sanity which had contributed to peace and security in the land for fifty years.

When the value system of a nation collapses in a time of catastrophic upheaval such as war or political revolution, the resultant changes in the patterns of human behaviour are staggering. People who were once good neighbours suddenly become fearsome enemies, as happened in the Rwanda inter-tribal atrocities which shocked the world in 1994 and 1995. Once the value system is disturbed it takes a long time to stabilise and become re-established. In other words, it takes much longer to establish stable norms in a society than it does to tear them apart.

In Britain during the second half of the twentieth century we have experienced a social revolution which has had a profound effect upon the norms and behaviour of the entire population. Although social historians agree that the 1960s was the decade of change, the seeds of change were already there in the immediate aftermath of World War Two. There was a desire for change, for the sweeping away of the old order dominated by tradition and a class system which was seen as being out of harmony with the development of the modern world.

The rising power of trades unions in this period, increased industrial output due to methods of production, full employment and rising wages which increased the purchasing power of the masses, all led to the explosion of social change in the 1960s. The rise of the pop culture in that decade, which changed Britain from a traditionally age-dominated society, was to have long-lasting effects. Young people with their new purchasing power not only had an effect upon the market in the production of consumer goods to suit their needs, but they also began to make an impact upon the political arena through demonstrations and the attention of the media, particularly through the rapid expansion of television which gave them instant publicity.

The anti-nuclear lobby became part of a powerful peace

movement linked to the calls for change, giving greater freedom to individual expression and choice. The slogan 'Make love, not war!' powerfully symbolised the spirit of the age. The drive to secure individual rights was linked to anti-racism and the calls for equality between the sexes. The slogan 'A woman's right to choose' escalated the legalisation of abortion. The demand for freedom in the arts swept away the restrictions on pornography and the public display of what previous generations had regarded as obscenity. That same demand for freedom led to the legalisation of homosexual acts between consenting males.

All these sweeping social changes and many more, such as the abolition of capital punishment and the easing of the divorce laws, were put onto the Statute Book by the British parliament in a remarkably short period. It is perhaps of some spiritual significance that even before the decade of the 1960s the very first measure approved by parliament, sweeping away tradition hundreds of years old, was the repeal of the Witchcraft Act in 1958. This not only legalised witchcraft practices and pagan rituals but also allowed the publication of a wide range of occult-related literature and materials. Thus the spiritual climate over the nation began to change before all the changes in social legislation were enacted. The legalisation of witch-craft helped to create a socially acceptable environment which prepared the way for the rise of fringe elements in the pop culture with its rock 'n' roll and heavy metal groups producing what some people claimed to be demon-ically inspired songs and sounds, with lyrics encouraging violence, subversion and anarchy.

Throughout this period of rapid social change the church appeared powerless and ineffective. Liberal theol-ogy reached the height of its popularity in this period with the teachings of Bultmann and Tillich undermining confidence in the Scriptures and producing thousands of preachers from liberal theological colleges who had no faith in a personal God and the uniqueness of the gospel. They were therefore at the mercy of the forces of change sweeping across the western world.

Dr John Robinson, the notorious Bishop of Woolwich, attacked traditional beliefs and values and was seen as the champion of the new free-thinking generation. His book of pop theology *Honest to God* became a bestseller. It brought to the wider public in simple language concepts which had been taught in theological colleges for decades. Robinson capped his attack upon traditional beliefs about God by appearing for the defence in the obscenity trial of *Lady Chatterley's Lover*, which paved the way for the flood of pornography which followed the relaxation of censorship relating to the public display of sex and violence.

The changes which took place in the 1960s have affected all our major social institutions and have affected the norms and behaviour of all those born since the middle of the century. It can be further argued that the lives of all citizens, including elderly people, have been affected in some way. Not only has family life radically changed with the movement from extended family, through nuclear family, to single-parent family, but the establishment of the welfare state has removed many of the functions performed by the family into the state arena. Notably the care of the elderly and the very young has become a primary responsibility carried by the state. Social workers have a statutory right to ensure the protection and wellbeing of children, while state homes and private nursing institutions take care of the elderly.

All these social changes reflect basic changes in the value system of the nation. But these changes in values were themselves preceded by changes in belief. In short, beliefs produce values, which determine norms, which govern behaviour. Thus the behavioural changes in each area of life can be traced backwards through these changes. For example, the trend in the 1990s for people simply to live together in an unmarried state is a behaviour pattern which stems from the norm which regards marriage as irrelevant. This in turn comes from the low regard with which we hold the value of personal commitment, loyalty and selfless love which regards the good of others more highly than the pursuit of self-interest. These values in turn stem from our fundamental beliefs in the sanctity of life, a life beyond death and personal accountability to God. Once this foundational belief in God is disturbed there is a chain reaction affecting values, norms and behaviour.

A biblical example illustrating this basic sociological construction may be seen in the Ten Commandments. The first commandment identifies God as the one and only true God.

This lays the foundation of fundamental belief. The second commandment is about idolatry. This establishes the value which flows out of the belief in one true God— you shall not make idols and bow down to worship them.

The third and fourth commandments are basic norms. They establish the norm that it is always wrong to misuse or blaspheme the name of God, and that the Sabbath should be kept as a holy day, a day set apart from the working week for the recognition of the central place of God in our lives.

The rest of the commandments are behavioural regulations—giving honour to our parents; respecting the sanctity of life and marriage; not harming our neighbour by stealing from him, lying about him or coveting his property.

It is of prime importance to understand this chain reaction, because it is integral to the process of social change

The process of social change

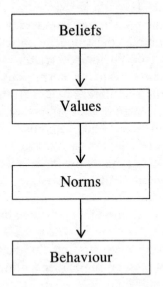

The chain reaction showing the primacy of beliefs in the formation of interventionist policies of creative social change

which we have been experiencing throughout the twentieth century. The following diagram illustrates this process.

The recognition of the way in which the processes of social change function in society is of prime importance in the construction of any interventionist policy. If we are to construct a policy of creative social change, for example, to slow down the rate of disintegration of family life in Britain, it is essential to understand how the processes of change work.

Let us consider an example. If the objective is to discourage young people from engaging in pre-marital sexual intercourse, it is not a bit of use deciding that girls should not be given the contraceptive pill without their parents' consent. That is an issue of *behaviour* which comes a long way down the chain reaction in the processes of change. If you want to change the behaviour of parents in their child-rearing practices, or the behaviour of teenagers in their courtship and sexual practices, *norms* have to be changed. So long as it is the norm for teenagers to engage in sexual experimentation the classroom conversation at school will be at the level of 'everybody's doing it' which creates a powerful peer pressure to conform. The issue of the availability or non-availability of contraception will not change sexual behaviour. It may indeed affect the number of teenage pregnancies but it will not reduce the number of young people engaging in sexual intercourse before marriage. The norm governing sexual behaviour is determined by the *value* placed upon the marriage which in turn comes from the regard or disregard for the *belief* in the sanctity of marriage. Thus, the right starting point to change the sexual behaviour of young people is with beliefs about marriage.

Secular academics specialising in the social sciences are familiar with the way in which these processes of social change function in society. Many sociologists, however, are atheistic or agnostic in personal belief and are often hostile towards religion, especially in their attitudes towards Christianity in the western world. They are therefore reluctant to admit the prime function of beliefs in the process of social change. Nevertheless Max Weber, one of the founding fathers of modern sociology, recognised the 'prophet' as a major source of creative social innovation. He saw the prophet as the herald of a new era, often calling people back to beliefs and values from the past which have been neglected. He also saw the prophet as actually formulating new ideas and concepts which usher in an era of change.

The Hebrew prophets of ancient Israel undoubtedly carried out this function. They were initiators of creative social change. Perhaps they knew more about the processes of social change than we imagine! Certainly their ministry was religious rather than social. They were not social reformers, yet social reform was the end product of their work. An excellent example is the ministry of the little-known prophet Azariah. King Asa of Judah was returning to Jerusalem following a resounding victory over a large army from Ethiopia which had invaded the southern borders of his territory. Following the battle in which the invaders had been routed, 'the men of Judah carried off a large amount of plunder . . . They also attacked the camps of the herdsmen and carried off droves of sheep and goats and camels' (2 Chron 14:12–15).

It was at this point that the prophet Azariah went out to meet the victorious army led by the king. He spoke straightly to them, warning them about the dangerous times in which they lived. He referred to the fact that 'it was not safe to travel about, for all the inhabitants of the lands were in great turmoil' (2 Chron 15:5). Presumably social conditions were similar in Judah because the prophet urged them to be strong and to work hard in seeking the Lord and obeying his commands.

The result of Azariah's prophecy was that the king initiated a policy of clearing idolatry out of the nation. 'He removed the detestable idols from the whole land of Judah and Benjamin and from the towns he had captured in the hills of Ephraim' (v 8). This clearly had a social effect which brought a period of peace and security to the kingdom which was so attractive that large numbers from the northern state of Israel migrated south to enjoy the benefits of living in Judah.

King Asa did not even allow family loyalties to hinder

his religious purge and he deposed his grandmother Maacah from her position as Queen Mother because she persisted in idolatrous practices, worshipping an Asherah pole (v 16).

Asa's first step in the process of national reform was to tackle the beliefs that were current in the nation. He not only tore down all the signs and symbols of idolatry but he also 'repaired the altar of the Lord that was in front of the portico of the Lord's temple' (v 8). This was the only altar which could be seen by the general populace, both Jew and non-Jew. This was a powerful symbol of the centrality of belief in God in the nation.

Asa's second step was to tackle the values in the nation. He summoned all the people together to a national assembly during which 'they entered into a covenant to seek the Lord, the God of their fathers, with all their heart and soul' (v 12). The effect of this was to turn away from idolatry and to reaffirm traditional values held by their ancestors and enshrined in the Torah and the teaching of the prophets. There was clearly a great sense of national unity because they all participated in this solemn reaffirmation of traditional values in a great public display of resolve, and 'all Judah rejoiced about the oath because they had sworn it whole-heartedly' (v 15).

The result of this change in belief and reaffirmation of traditional values was a change in the norms among the people which was attractive enough to encourage people to settle in Judah from neighbouring states. Finally, these changes clearly brought about a change in behaviour among the people. The account in 2 Chronicles 15 is tantalisingly terse and short on detail. It simply records, 'They sought God eagerly, and he was found by them. So the Lord gave them rest on every side' (v 15). This evidently refers to internal peace and harmony within the state of Judah because it is elsewhere in the account (v 19) that we are told the international situation—for a number of years there was no more war.

If the beliefs of a nation are, as we contend, the prime agent in determining values and thereby affecting norms and behaviour, then the role of the church in influencing the beliefs of the nation becomes of paramount social as well as spiritual significance. If the church was functioning as the prophet to the nation she would not only be giving warnings of the danger due, for example to the disintegration of stable family life in Britain, but also pointing the way to an alternative standard of family life based upon the biblical model, which in turn comes from a belief in God.

The biblical model of the family provides a strong contrast to the loneliness and lack of support for the individual seen in Britain today. The biblical family provides support and security for everyone.

We referred in Chapter 8 to the solidarity of the family in ancient Israel which consisted of three generations, grandparents, parents and children, linked to a clan, linked to a tribe and part of the nation. Each individual had the security of knowing that he or she belonged to a family that was part of a nation which was in a covenant relationship with God. In fact the whole nation was seen as one large family under God so that the prophets were able to bring the word of God to them in those terms. Hosea, for example, could speak of God's love for all his people as a father loves his children: 'When Israel was a child I loved him and out of Egypt I called my son' (Hos 11:1).

The Hebrew understanding of the family was carried over by the apostles into the New Testament church. Paul saw the church as one family under 'Abba, Father' with Jesus the 'first-born son'. He referred to the church as 'the family of believers' (Gal 6:10). Similarly, Peter referred to the church as 'the family of God' (1 Pet 4:17). It is this model of the church as a family that could be of immense value in today's climate of family disintegration.

If western society is to survive we have to pay attention to the desperate plight of the family and begin to rebuild family life according to the pattern God has given us in the Bible. This provides the principles upon which the family could be remodelled in the context of modern society. These could form the basis for a model in which every individual of any age, from birth to old age, can be guarded against loneliness, given support, security and loving care. But such a basic social change cannot be brought about simply by regarding the three-generational model of the family as the ideal for a healthy society. There are millions of sceptics in Britain today who would rubbish such a contention and pour scorn upon what they would see as a reactionary attempt to reintroduce the traditional concept of the family. The traditional family is regarded by many today as an oppressive unit curtailing the freedom of the individual to live according to his own individual norms and to satisfy his own desires.

In order to create the right social climate for the advocacy of the biblical model of the family its value must first be established, and this in turn is an outcome of a belief in God, of our accountability to him, of his nature as the Father who cares for his children and of his purposes which are for good and not for evil. Jeremiah expressed this beautifully in a letter to the exiles in Babylon, reassuring them that God had not forgotten them: '"For I know the plans I have for you," declares the Lord, "plans to prosper you and not to harm you, plans to give you hope and a future"' (Jer 29:11).

Similarly, if our other major social institutions, alongside the family, such as the economy and education, are to be radically changed, then the right place to begin is with the values held within each institution. We shall come back to our contention that values themselves are derived from the belief system in society. Nevertheless, within each institution the underlying values are the right starting point for institutional reform.

For example, within the economy, if basic changes are to be made the right starting point is to ask: What are the values held by industry and commerce and by those who work within these institutions, both management and workers? Reference has already been made to the 'quality movement' initiated by the Japanese and now being widely adopted within the western industrialised nations. This movement recognises the primacy of values in determining the efficiency of an organisation in carrying out its objectives.

A major problem which has bedevilled the British economy since the days of the Industrial Revolution has been the conflict of interest between workers and management. This became institutionalised in the nineteenth century in the trades union movement and has led to innumerable periods of conflict, strikes and even violence. The basic problem is a conflict of interest between management and workers; management seeking to maximise profits and minimise costs, including that of labour, and workers seeking more money in their pockets and better working conditions. Sadly the two have rarely perceived these objectives as providing common ground for co-operation. Clearly, if there were a shared set of values instead of greed and exploitation on one side and narrow self-interest on the other, industry and commerce would benefit and the whole economy would be much healthier. Such a concept of shared values in the pursuit of goals and objectives leading to the common good is yet to become generally accepted in western capitalist economies driven, as they are, by the profit motive. The huge salaries paid to management executives are both an affront and a constant irritant to workers on low wages and others on fixed incomes.

In terms of education, the 1990s have seen a renewed emphasis upon values in the face of a growing public outcry concerning what has been seen as falling standards of education and rising rates of juvenile crime. The behavioural problems of children in schools have been a concern both of parents and educational authorities. Many teachers have suffered violence at the hands of children and, in the face of falling recruitment and an increase in the number of teachers taking early retirement, the public debate has focused upon the whole range of standards within schools. In 1993 66,000 children were excluded from schools in the UK for behavioural reasons. These children soon become involved in petty crime or more serious criminal activities such as stealing cars, or they become an easy target for drug pushers and older criminals.

The majority of parents are concerned about the values which influence their children, about standards of behaviour in schools, and about all aspects of their children's educational and personality development. Fresh importance has been given to the matter in the 1990s through government policy requiring schools' inspectors to keep the Secretary of State informed about 'spiritual, moral, social and cultural development of pupils at schools'. This requirement was written into the Government White Paper, '*Choice and Diversity—a framework for schools*' (Department of Education, 1992). Chapter eight of this paper made an astounding statement which reversed the educational and social trends of the 1960s. It stated, '*Education cannot and must not be value free*,' and stressed the need to teach spiritual, moral, social and cultural values in schools. It proposed regulations requiring schools to publish information concerning their 'set of shared values which is promoted through the curriculum, through expectations governing the behaviour of pupils and staff and through day-to-day contact between them'.

The post-World-War-Two period, which saw the rise of the philosophy of 'value freedom' in education and child development, has clearly been recognised for the disastrous policy that it is. Value freedom results in moral anarchy. It opens the door to the exploitation of the young and vulnerable. It results in the predominance of the lowest common moral denominator. It is a simple fact of life that where there are no norms or guidelines for behaviour established by clearly defined values, sinful human nature always ensures that the worst standards of behaviour prevail. Christians recognise this as a consequence of the Fall, that our human nature has a fundamental propensity towards the pursuit of self-interest, violence, greed and the exploitation of others.

Government policy, which recognises the importance of values for child development within the educational system, is greatly to be welcomed. But the question then arises as to how such values can be inculcated into local schools if they are not firmly held as part of the personal convictions of the teachers and staff within the schools. If a set of values, however lofty, is imposed from the outside and not shared by the teachers, they will not be able to teach them to the children and certainly their own lifestyles and behaviour will not reflect the values officially promoted within the school. We come, therefore, back to the need for the creation of the right moral and spiritual environment in which values may flourish and our contention that this is created by the right belief system.

This brings us to a consideration of the process whereby beliefs, values, norms and behavioural patterns are transmitted from one generation to the next, which is known to the sociologist as the process of socialisation. In a modern western industrialised society the four major institutions involved in this process of transmission are: the family, education, peer groups, and the media.

In order to change the value system of a society, all four of these institutions need to be channelling their influence towards a common end. Clearly, if families and schools agree to teach a common set of values but the media portray values which are diametrically opposed, this will result in widespread confusion, particularly for children and young people who do not yet have their values formed. Peer group pressure is of considerable importance in reinforcing norms and regulating the behaviour of individuals, but the peer group values are themselves derived from the family, education and the media. These three are the major influences in modern society. But from where do they derive their values? This is the fundamental question and brings us back to our original contention of the primacy of beliefs.

The belief system of a nation acts as an overarching conceptual framework from which the values of that nation are derived. To change the metaphor—our beliefs are like the subsoil underneath the foundations of a building. These foundations are the values upon which the whole social structure is built. If the belief system of a nation is to be changed, that has to be the responsibility of those who hold strong religious convictions. It is therefore our contention that the church carries the major responsibility for initiating policies of creative social change and reform which begin, not with hand-wringing exhortations about behaviour, but by teaching fundamental truths concerning the nature and purposes of God, his purposes underlying creation and his provision for the whole family of humankind.

This is the starting point of social and moral reform and the right point of entry for interventionist policies promoting creative social change. All other policies are doomed to failure because they are not based upon an understanding of the processes of change which have been sweeping across the world throughout the twentieth century. In the next chapters we shall examine more closely the biblical principles involved in a policy of creative change and the role of the church as prophet to the nations.

10

Biblical Principles

Moral and spiritual values in Scripture are derived from the fundamental source of creation, namely from God himself. A major task of the prophets from the time of Moses through to Malachi was to reveal to Israel the nature and purposes of God. Prophecy is, by biblical definition, 'revelation'. The prophets who received revelation were not dependent upon human intellect or wisdom but upon the self-revelation of God. In the account of the call of Samuel to the prophetic ministry we read, 'Samuel did not yet know the Lord; the word of the Lord had not yet been *revealed* to him.' And then, after God had spoken to him, it is said, 'The Lord continued to appear at Shiloh, and there he *revealed* himself to Samuel through his word' (1 Sam 3:7, 21, emphasis mine).

It was this revelation of God to his servants the prophets which gave them their distinctive message as well as their power and authority. When they spoke the word of God the prophets were not orators, they were messengers; when they wrote the word they were not authors, they were scribes.

There were two ways in which God revealed his word to the prophets: through his *deeds* and through his *words*.

God was known as a God of action. His deeds revealed his nature and through his activity among the nations and espe-

cially among his covenant people he fulfilled his purposes, so
that his deeds revealed both his nature and purposes. Psalm
106 beautifully expresses the activity of God among his
people which reveals his nature:

> The Lord works righteousness and justice for all the oppressed.
> He made known his ways to Moses, his deeds to the people of
> Israel; the Lord is compassionate and gracious, slow to anger,
> abounding in love . . . He does not treat us as our sins deserve
> or repay us according to our iniquities (vv 6–10).

The prophets constantly reminded the people of God's
activity in history. He was known as a Saviour by the way
he had heard the cries of the Israelites in slavery and had
acted to save them from suffering and to deliver them out
of the hands of their oppressors. The prophets lost no
opportunity of reminding the people of God's gracious
deliverance of their forefathers as a preface to bringing
a word of rebuke. A good example is Hosea 13:4f:

> I am the Lord your God who brought you out of Egypt . . . I
> cared for you in the desert in the land of burning heat. When I
> fed them they were satisfied; when they were satisfied, they
> became proud; then they forgot me. So I will come upon them
> like a lion . . .

It was in the context of the activity of God in the world
and the recognition that he was known by his deeds that
the prophets were able to bring the word of God to the
people relative to contemporary events. Thus Jeremiah
was able to say that the reason why the spring and autumn
rains had been withheld was because of the sins of the
people (v 25). Similarly, Amos used a string of local
events which would have been known to his hearers. He
referred to famine, drought, crop diseases, plagues and
defeats in battle, saying that God had allowed each of
these to occur as a sign to the people. Following each

example the prophet added the words, '"Yet you have not returned to me," declares the Lord' (Amos 4:6–12).

It was not only through his deeds that God communicated his word to his servants the prophets; he also spoke to them. Moses was said to have spoken with God face to face (Num 12:8). It was to Moses that the Decalogue (Ten Commandments) and much of the teaching, the Torah, were given. The Decalogue in Deuteronomy 5 is central to the biblical revelation of moral and spiritual values. It summarises the ethical requirements of God for his people.

> You shall have no other gods before me
> You shall not make for yourself an idol
> You shall not misuse the name of the Lord your God
> Remember the Sabbath day by keeping it holy
> Honour your father and your mother
> You shall not murder
> You shall not commit adultery
> You shall not steal
> You shall not give false testimony
> You shall not covet

The first three commandments all relate to our attitude to God, while the rest relate to our attitude towards other people and our activity in society. They are regulations for personal and social morality, relating to the private and public spheres of human behaviour. Rightly perceived, all these regulations are for the health and well-being of the individual and for the good of the community. It is clearly good for our minds and bodies to rest one day in seven. It creates healthy attitudes of respect in society for parents to be honoured. A society where there is respect for life, marriage, property and truthfulness is a society where the well-being and security of each individual are assured. The final warning against covetousness is clearly for the health of the individual.

One of the modern objections to the Ten Commandments is that most of them are expressed negatively. Yet if we stop and think how we teach young children it is usually in the same way. We say, 'Don't touch that or you will be hurt!' or, 'Don't go too near the fire,' or, 'Don't run into the road.' These negative commands are given to the child as strong warnings of danger. That is why they are expressed negatively and as imperatives. It is necessary for the child's health and well-being that he should accept these directives and obey them. If he disobeys and runs into the road he could be severely injured or killed. In the same way, God as a loving Father teaches his children the basic requirements for their health, safety and well-being. Thus the first requirement is a right attitude to God and then right attitudes towards other people in the family and in the community. These are essential not only for individual well-being and security, but for the very survival of the community and the nation.

In order to have a right understanding of biblical principles, it is essential to grasp the context in which they are presented. God's requirements of his people flow out of his own nature. It is because God himself is holy that he requires holiness of his people. God is faithful and keeps his promises; he entered a covenant with his people, not because they were the greatest or were his favourites, but because he chose them from among the nations to be his servant. Therefore God expected his people to be faithful, to keep their promises and not break the covenant. It is not possible to appreciate the revelation of the word of God through the prophets without first having a clear picture of the nature of God in their understanding. Their teaching of the requirements of God stems from this understanding. They saw him as a God of *constancy*, a God of *love*, a God of *mercy*, a God of *justice*, a God of *holiness*, a God of *faithfulness* and a God of *truth*. It is these concepts of God which form the basis of biblical principles and therefore form an ethic of society covering both personal and public morality.

Constancy

The God of biblical revelation is not a capricious God like the false gods of the other nations. He is totally reliable, dependable and consistent. It was this self-consistency in the nature of God which provided the foundation for the ministry of the prophets of Israel. They knew that God would never deny himself; that what he called 'good' on one occasion he would still call 'good' hundreds of years later. What he declared to be evil would always be evil.

God did not act in an arbitrary manner like the fickle Baals of the Canaanites or the gods of the surrounding nations who often demanded detestable practices from their people, such as the god of Molech who required infant sacrifice. Jeremiah gives powerful expression to this absolute dependability of God. Many of the people were already in exile in Babylon but he foresaw the day when God would restore them to the land and—despite the unfaithfulness of the people which resulted in exile, the destruction of Jerusalem and the scattering of the people among the nations—God would never break his covenant with them. He refers to the God who had appointed the sun to shine by day and 'who decrees the moon and stars to shine by night' and he says, '"Only if these decrees vanish from my sight," declares the Lord, "will the descendants of Israel ever cease to be a nation before me"' (Jer 31:35–36).

Despite more than 2,500 years of oppression and cruelty which the Jews have suffered at the hands of those who hate them, and despite being scattered across all the nations of the world, they have never lost their identity as a nation—the descendants of Israel. This solemn promise has been literally fulfilled, which is quite amazing in view of the many centuries that have passed and in the face of all that has happened to them over such a long period of history. Clearly God intended that promise to stand for ever as he reinforced it with the declaration, '"Only if the heavens above can be measured and the foundations of the earth below be searched out will I reject all the descendants of Israel because of all they have done," declares the Lord' (v 37).

It is in the light of this utter dependability of God and his faithfulness in keeping his promise to restore the descendants of Israel to the land and in keeping his covenant with them despite their unfaithfulness, that Gentile believers, who have come into a right relationship with him through the New Covenant, may trust him to keep his word and depend upon him to keep his covenant with them. If God could not be trusted to keep his covenant with Israel he could not be trusted to keep his covenant with Gentile believers. It was the self-consistency and utter dependability of God which enabled the prophets to predict with confidence what God would do in different situations and to declare his word with conviction and authority.

Love

All the way through the Bible God is described as a God of love. Moses said, 'The Lord is slow to anger, abounding in love and forgiving sin and rebellion' (Num 14:18). The love of God is referred to scores of times throughout the Psalms. The psalmists continually rejoiced in the love of God, 'How priceless is your unfailing love!' (36:7); 'You are forgiving and good, O Lord, abounding in love to all who call to you' (86:5); and the declaration, 'His love endures for ever!' is the recurring theme of Psalm 136.

The prophets spoke of the love of God for his people.

Hosea expresses this as the tender compassion of God which is like a loving father caring for a small child: 'It waş I who taught Ephraim to walk, taking them by the arm; but they did not realise it was I who healed them. I led them with cords of human kindness, with ties of love' (11:3–4).

In the post-exilic period God was seen as actually entering into the suffering of his people. 'In all their distress he too was distressed, and the angel of his presence saved them. In his love and mercy he redeemed them' (Is 63:9). This love of God was not just something theoretical, it was to be seen in the deeds of the Lord: 'I will tell of the kindnesses of the Lord, the deeds for which he is to be praised . . . the many good things he has done for the house of Israel, according to his compassion' (Is 63:7).

God demonstrated his love for his people by becoming their Saviour, which is the constant theme of the New Testament. The witness of Jesus was that 'God so loved the world that he gave his one and only Son, that whoever believes in him shall not perish but have eternal life' (Jn 3:16). Paul rejoiced that God's love is given to us unconditionally: 'But God demonstrates his own love for us in this: While we were still sinners, Christ died for us' (Rom 5:8). It was because love is part of the very nature of God that he calls for a response of love from his people.

Mercy

This is another basic biblical principle which comes from the very nature of God who is merciful. He continually shows mercy to those who richly deserve punishment. The eighth-century prophet Micah was well aware of the sins of the nation. Everywhere he went he saw injustice, deceit, bribery and corruption, divination and idolatry (Mic 3:11); but nevertheless, although he foresaw disaster if the nation did not repent, he believed in the mercy of God and his willingness to forgive sin. He said:

> Who is a God like you, who pardons sin and forgives the transgression of the remnant of his inheritance? You do not stay angry for ever but delight to show mercy. You will again have compassion on us; you will tread our sins under foot (7:18).

It was because the mercy of God was demonstrated in his deeds, his forgiveness, his compassion and loving-kindness towards his people despite their sinfulness that the prophets were able to say that God requires mercy in his people in all their dealings with one another. Jesus made this explicit when he said, 'Be merciful just as your Father is merciful' (Lk 6:36).

Justice and righteousness

The theme of justice runs right the way through the Bible. 'The Lord is known by his justice' (Ps 9:16); 'I will sing of your love and justice' (Ps 101:1). Isaiah declared that 'the Lord is a God of justice' (30:18); 'I will make justice the measuring line' (28:17) and, 'My justice will become a light to the nations' (51:4).

It was because God was a God of justice that he required justice among his people. Jesus rebuked the Pharisees because they paid careful attention to the minutiae of the law but neglected the great commandments. 'You give God a tenth of your mint, rue and other kinds of garden herbs, but neglect justice and the love of God' (Lk 11:42).

Isaiah speaks of God as a God of justice but he also links this with his mercy and his desire to show compassion to his sinful and rebellious people. He says, 'The Lord longs to be gracious to you; he rises to show you compassion. For the Lord is a God of justice' (Is 30:18). In the teaching of the prophets there is no contradiction in linking God's compassion with his justice. But this throws into sharp relief the difference between the Hebrew understanding of justice and our western concept. Modern western thought is derived from the Roman understanding of justice which is legalistic and based on retribution. Roman justice demanded that the punishment fitted the crime. Thus, for God to be merciful and to have compassion upon a sinful people would have been a denial of his justice which demands punishment. Retributive justice cannot be satisfied until the full price has been paid for the wrongdoing.

In contrast to the Roman concept of justice, the Hebrew prophets and teachers thought of justice in terms of relationships, and God's relationships with men and women are always based upon mercy. The just man in Hebrew thinking was the one who was in a right relationship with God and with his neighbours. Hence love and mercy long to have compassion upon the penitent sinner and to restore him to a right relationship with the one from whom he is estranged by reason of his wrongdoing. That wrongdoing breaks harmonious relationships which are based upon love and trust. This is what Isaiah meant when he said that God 'looked for justice, but saw bloodshed; for righteousness, but heard cries of distress' (5:7). God was looking for right relationships among his people but he saw only violence and oppression.

God would have been perfectly justified in allowing disaster to come upon his people who had broken the covenant and therefore severed right relationships with him. Isaiah went further. He saw that for God to allow destruction and exile to come upon his people who had turned the moral law upside down and called 'evil good and good evil' (5:20) would actually be a demonstration to the world of his justice. 'The Lord Almighty will be exalted by his justice, and the holy God will show himself holy by his righteousness' (5:16).

Sin broke the bond of right relationships with God and that broken relationship could only be restored by the penitence of the sinner and the forgiveness of God.

It was this deep desire to restore men and women to right relationships with himself that prompted God, in the fullness of time, to send his only Son into the world to save men and women from the consequences of their own sinfulness and to bring them into a new covenant of righteousness with himself. Jesus himself said:

> For God did not send his Son into the world to condemn the world, but to save the world through him. Whoever believes in him is not condemned, but whoever does not believe stands condemned already because he has not believed in the name of God's one and only Son (Jn 3:17–18).

Paul related God's act of redemption to his justice and righteousness—interchangeable terms in Paul's Hebrew theology. He says, 'This righteousness from God comes through faith in Jesus Christ and to all who believe . . . God presented him as a sacrifice of atonement, through faith in his blood. He did this to demonstrate his justice' (Rom 3:21–25).

It is because of what God has done in bringing sinful men and women into a right relationship with himself through Christ that he is able to expect men and women to treat each other with justice and righteousness. So Paul exhorts believers, 'Count yourselves dead to sin but alive to God in Christ Jesus . . . Offer yourselves to God, as those who have been brought from death to life; and offer the parts of your body to him as instruments of righteousness' (Rom 6:11–13).

Part of our problem in understanding biblical principles is the contrasting mindset between our modern western thinking and that of the Hebrew prophets and teachers. We like everything to be neat and to come to a logical conclusion. The Hebrew sages, on the other hand, were quite content to have ragged ends to their theological precepts. They did not try to tie up all the loose ends. They were quite happy to leave two apparently contradictory statements unresolved. They could say, for example, that God is a God of justice who demands full punishment of the sinner: God is a God of mercy who freely forgives the sinner and does not hold his transgressions against him.

To the Roman concept of justice that was nonsense and it had to be resolved one way or the other. Hence the endless debates about the meaning of the Atonement in Christian theology from the time of the early church fathers until today. But for the Hebrew there was no problem. God may choose to exercise mercy; he may choose to punish. Either way he is a God of justice. Either way he is a God of mercy. This Hebrew way of theological thinking, which is so foreign to us, is clearly to be seen in Paul who breaks into a song of praise when he says that no one can understand the ways of God—'How unsearchable his judgments, and his paths beyond tracing out! Who has known the mind of the Lord?' (Rom 11:33–36).

Holiness

Isaiah was overwhelmed with the experience of God's holiness when he received his call to the prophetic ministry. 'Holy, holy, holy is the Lord God Almighty.' The words immediately reminded Isaiah of his own uncleanness and unworthiness. '"Woe to me!" I cried. "I am ruined! For I am a man of unclean lips"' (6:3–5). Isaiah was overwhelmed by a sense of awe that he should be privileged to be allowed to enter the presence of the living God who was sinless and 'wholly other' from the material creation and the people of unclean lips among whom he lived. Although God was unapproachable by sinful people and entirely set apart from the profane things of this world, in his love and compassion for the men and women whom he had created, God communicated with them and showed them the way to enter into a right relationship with him and to walk in love and harmony with one another which is pleasing in his sight.

One of the tasks of spiritual leaders is to teach holiness. God gave a solemn commandment to the priests of Israel in this duty. He declared it to be 'a lasting ordinance for generations to come. You must distinguish between the holy and the common, between the unclean and the clean, and you must teach the Israelites all the decrees the Lord has given them through Moses' (Lev 10:10–11). Ezekiel speaks of God as being outraged by those in positions of leadership who did not do this. 'Her priests do violence to my law and profane my holy things; they do not distinguish between the holy and the common; they teach that there is no difference between the unclean and the clean' (Ezek 22:26).

Paul, writing to Timothy, exhorted him to live a holy life. He said that the God who has saved us has 'called us to a holy life—not because of anything we have done but because of his purpose and grace' (2 Tim 1:9). God's purpose in calling his people to be holy is that they should be different from others. They should be separate from the world, not in a physical sense, but in lifestyle. In other words they should love the values of the kingdom of God and not the values of the world. That is the essential characteristic of the biblical concept of holiness.

Faithfulness

From the earliest point in the history of the nation God was known to Israel as a faithful God. This is how Moses taught the people: 'Know therefore that the Lord your God is God; he is the faithful God, keeping his covenant of love to a thousand generations of those who love him and keep his commands' (Deut 7:9). Many of the Psalms speak of God as the faithful one who keeps his promises and who remains faithful for ever. The faithfulness of God is a theme running right the way through Scripture, especially in the songs of praise and rejoicing sung by David and others who composed the songs of Israel. Isaiah, in a Messianic passage describing the coming Redeemer, said, 'Righteousness will be his belt and faithfulness the sash round his waist' (11:5).

Among the eighth-century prophets Hosea dwelt at length upon the faithfulness of God. Although he saw 'no faithfulness, no love, no acknowledgment of God in the land' (4:1) God nevertheless remained faithful. His promise was, 'I will betroth you in faithfulness' (2:20). Hosea saw the faithlessness of Israel in contrast to the faithfulness of God as an almost unbelievable tragedy. God had loved Israel since the childhood of the nation, fed him, healed him, protected and cared for him in every way. But instead of responding to the love and faithfulness of God the prophet said, 'Ephraim has surrounded me with lies, the house of Israel with deceit, and Judah is unruly against God, even against the faithful holy one' (11:12).

Despite the lies, deceit and faithlessness of the nation who had entered into a solemn covenant with God, he remained faithful and promised, 'I will ransom them from the power of the grave; I will redeem them from death . . . I will heal their waywardness and love them freely' (13:14; 14:4).

It was because the prophets knew that faithfulness was part of the very nature of God that they were able to declare his good purposes for the nation even in the face of national tragedy such as the destruction of Jerusalem. Jeremiah spoke with great confidence that God would watch over his people, even those who were in slavery in Babylon. The day would come when he would bring them back to the land of Judah. The faithfulness of God was such that he had good plans for his people (29:11) and Jeremiah could foresee the day coming when the towns of Judah and the streets of Jerusalem which were at present deserted would once more be filled with the 'sounds of joy and gladness' and the people would be bringing their thank-offerings to the house of the Lord saying, 'Give thanks to the Lord Almighty for he is good; his love endures for ever' (33:11).

Truth

Throughout the Bible truth is upheld as one of the funda-mental principles or values associated with God. Truth was part of the very nature of God. Isaiah 65:16 refers to God as 'the God of truth'. He looks forward to the time when there will be justice and righteousness in the land and 'whoever invokes a blessing in the land will do so by the God of truth'. Many of the Psalms also refer to God in the same way: 'Into your hands I commit my spirit; redeem me, O Lord, the God of truth' (31:5). The psal-mist's prayer in 40:11 is, 'Do not withhold your mercy from me, O Lord; may your love and your truth always protect me.' A similar prayer is, 'Teach me your way, O Lord, and I will walk in your truth' (86:11).

It is because God is truth and he speaks the truth that he requires his people to do likewise. 'I, the Lord, speak the truth; I declare what is right' (Is 45:19). The God of truth and righteousness grieves when his people break the covenant relationship with him: 'So justice is driven back, and righteousness stands at a distance; truth has stumbled in the streets, honesty cannot enter. Truth is nowhere to be found ... The Lord looked and was displeased . . . he was appalled that there was no-one to intercede' (Is 59:14–16). The prophet saw the inevitable consequences of destruction falling upon those who have deliberately turned away from truth and righteousness.

The same standard of truth as a mark of the kingdom is found throughout the teaching of Jesus. In fact Jesus, who inaugurated the kingdom, was himself the embodiment of truth. In the prologue of John which is his account of the incarnation he describes Jesus as the one 'who came from the Father, full of grace and truth' (Jn 1:14). Jesus described himself in John 14:5 as 'the way and the truth and the life'. Throughout the Gospels a favourite saying of Jesus is 'I tell you the truth'. He was constantly emphasising the truth which he had come from the Father to reveal to those who would accept his witness and receive his word. He described the Spirit of God as the Spirit of truth whom the world cannot accept because the values of the kingdom of God are so contrary to the values of the world (Jn 14:17).

The teaching of the apostles also places great emphasis upon truth. Paul refers to the gospel as being 'the word of truth' (Col 1:5) and he urges Timothy to be careful in handling the word of truth (2 Tim 2:15) while in 2 Thessalonians 2 he refers to the times of lawlessness preceding the Second Coming of Christ and says that in those days there will be great deception because people will turn away from the love of truth. 'A powerful delusion' will come upon them. People will believe lies. Paul says that 'all will be condemned who have not believed the truth but have delighted in wickedness' (v 12).

In the teaching of both Jesus and the apostles those who deliberately reject the gospel are guilty of rejecting truth and embracing the lies of the world. To reject the truth is to reject not only the word of God, but God himself since he is truth, and Jesus, as the incarnation of God, is the Word made flesh—the way, the truth and the life.

The unchanging God

It was because the prophets had such a firm belief in the unchangeable nature of God that they were able to declare his word with such utter conviction. The declaration in Isaiah 43:12, 'I have revealed and saved and proclaimed' was the foundation underlying the ministry of all the biblical prophets. There was only one God who was the Creator of the whole universe and it was he who had revealed himself to the prophets both through his saving acts and through his word which they proclaimed. 'Before me no God was formed nor will there be one after me . . . Apart from me there is no Saviour' (Is 43:10–11). Samuel emphasised the unchangeable nature of God in his dispute with Saul: 'He who is the glory of Israel does not lie or change his mind; for he is not a man, that he should change his mind' (1 Sam 15:29). And in Malachi 3:6 we find the definitive statement, 'I the Lord do not change.'

From this understanding of the unchanging nature of God the prophets were able to declare two facts of immense significance which run right the way through the Bible from the Pentateuch to Revelation; they are the unchanging purposes of God and his unchanging requirements of his people. It was a major task of the prophets to discern the purposes of God and the way in which he was working them out in each generation. Hence Jeremiah was able to send a message from God to the exiles in Babylon, '"I know the plans I have for you," declares the Lord, "plans to prosper you and not to harm you, plans to give you hope and a future"' (29:11). And similarly Isaiah, more than a century earlier, had warned the leaders of Judah against forming alliances with foreign nations without consulting God and discerning what his plans for them were at that time: '"Woe to the obstinate children," declares the Lord, "to those who carry out plans that are not mine"' (30:1).

The ministry of the prophets was to declare the purposes of God to the nation. But first they themselves had to learn to enter the presence of God in order to receive his word. The false prophets cared for none of these things and were usually more concerned to bring a popular word to the people. Hence Micah complains, 'If a liar and deceiver comes and says, "I will prophesy for you plenty of wine and beer," he would be just the prophet for this people!' (2:11). And in Jeremiah 23:18 we read, 'But which of them has stood in the counsel of the Lord to see or to hear his word?' And in verse 22 there is the devastating indictment from God, 'If they had stood in my counsel, they would have proclaimed my words to my people and would have turned them from their evil ways and from their evil deeds.'

Jeremiah himself did not hesitate to proclaim fearlessly and in public the word he was hearing from God, even though he knew it would be hated and rejected by the people.

The clearest example of Jeremiah's preaching is in chapter 7 where he was told to stand at the entrance to the Temple and proclaim a message which was both a strong warning and a call to repentance. It began with the call 'Reform your ways and your actions,' which was followed by a strong condemnation of the six sins of Jerusalem which were abhorrent to God:

(1) false religion
(2) injustice
(3) oppression
(4) violence and murder
(5) idolatry
(6) immorality.

In a few terse sentences in verses 4–9, Jeremiah gives a vivid description of the moral and spiritual anarchy in the city where there was idolatry in the streets of Jerusalem involving people of all ages: 'The children gather wood, the fathers light the fire, and the women knead the dough and make cakes of bread for the Queen of Heaven' (v 18). There was injustice, oppression, lying, stealing and adultery. In the midst of all this the people had a blind faith that because of the presence of the Temple, God would never allow disaster to happen to Jerusalem. The prophet almost exploded that the people should dare to do all these things which were directly contrary to the word of God and then come into the Temple which bore his name, 'and say, "We are safe"—safe to do all these detestable things? Has this house, which bears my Name, become a den of robbers to you? But I have been watching! declares the Lord' (vv 10–11).

Eternal values

The Torah (what we call 'the Law' in our English Bibles) and the prophets form the background for the moral and the spiritual teaching of Jesus and the apostles in the New Testament. Although Jesus' teaching is distinctive and his emphases are different from those who were the teachers of Israel in his day, nevertheless constancy is part of the nature of God and God does not deny his word. If he declares something to be sinful in one generation it will always be sinful, even thousands of years later. In the Deuteronomic code homosexual practices were declared to be detestable to God, hence we find Paul emphasising precisely the same teaching when writing to the believers in Rome many hundreds of years later (Rom 1:24f).

Jesus states emphatically that he did not come to destroy the Torah or the prophets but to fulfil them (Mt

5:17). He followed this with a clear statement that none of the word of God would disappear until the whole purposes of God have been accomplished. Thus he said, 'Anyone who breaks one of the least of these commandments and teaches others to do the same will be called least in the kingdom' (Mt 5:19).

Much of Jesus' teaching concerned the values of the kingdom of God and norms of behaviour derived from them. In many ways he strengthened rather than undermined the Torah; for example, statements such as this: 'You have heard that it was said, "Do not commit adultery." But I tell you that anyone who looks at a woman lustfully has already committed adultery with her in his heart' (Mt 5:27–28).

In other instances Jesus reinterpreted traditional teaching, making mercy more important than retribution as, for example, in Matthew 5:38, 'You have heard that it was said, "Eye for eye, and tooth for tooth." But I tell you, Do not resist an evil person. If someone strikes you on the right cheek, turn him the other also.' Similarly, he extended the teaching on love to become a universal command not only to love those whom we like: 'You have heard that it was said, "Love your neighbour and hate your enemy." But I tell you: Love your enemies and pray for those who persecute you, that you may be sons of your Father in heaven' (Mt 5:43).

Jesus' teaching is consistent with the seven basic characteristics of the nature of God revealed through the prophets. His special emphases reflect the errors in the teaching given by the religious leaders in his own day or values to which they were giving insufficient emphasis; hence Jesus constantly referred to the love of God, his mercy and his faithfulness in forgiving the penitent sinner.

The apostles similarly emphasised the fundamental values of the kingdom of God as taught by Jesus, which were different from the values of the world. Paul chided the Colossians, 'Since you died with Christ to the basic principles of this world, why, as though you still belonged to it, do you submit to its rules?' (Col 2:20). He went on to pour scorn upon those values which 'are based on human commands and teachings'. He urged the believers to 'put to death, therefore, whatever belongs to your earthly nature; sexual immorality, impurity, lust, evil desires and greed, which is idolatry. Because of these things, the wrath of God is coming' (Col 3:5–6).

Paul did not just condemn worldly values and standards of behaviour, he also emphasised the positive: 'Clothe yourselves with compassion, kindness, humility, gentleness and patience . . . Forgive as the Lord forgave you. And over all these virtues put on love' (Col 3:12–14).

In his teaching on the values linked with the kingdom of God, Paul usually contrasts them with the values of the world so that, on the one hand, he warns against giving way to what he calls 'the desires of the sinful nature' (Gal 5:16) which he lists in verses 19–21 with an emphatic warning, 'I warn you, as I did before, that those who live like this will not inherit the kingdom of God,' but he follows this with the positive statement that 'the fruit of the Spirit is love, joy, peace, patience, kindness, goodness, faithfulness, gentleness and self-control'.

Paul's teaching on holiness encourages believers to be separate from the world in terms of not sharing worldly values. Such teaching is based upon the fact that God is holy, separated from the common and the unclean which are all characteristics of the world.

Throughout the New Testament, both in the teaching of Jesus and that of the apostles, there is strong emphasis upon truth which is also part of the very nature of God. In one of the strongest passages in any of his letters Paul warns about the wrath of God 'being revealed from heaven against all the godlessness and wickedness of men who suppress the truth by their wickedness' (Rom 1:18). He argues that God's truth has been plainly revealed for all men and women to perceive. If they fail to embrace the truth it is because they have deliberately rejected truth and been driven by the desires of their sinful nature, thus putting themselves in rebellion against God.

Paul says it is because of this deliberate rebellion against God that he eventually 'gave them over in the sinful desires of their hearts to sexual impurity for the degrading of their bodies with one another. They exchanged the truth of God for a lie, and worshipped and served created things rather than the Creator' (Rom 1:24–25). It is this statement that sinful men and women have exchanged the truth of God for a lie that is so significant in Paul's teaching about the values of the kingdom. He repeats the phrase 'God gave them over' in verses 26 and 28, thus emphasising God's abhorrence of the actions of those who deliberately turn away from the truth and embrace values which lead to the destruction of their bodies, to 'greed and depravity' distorting their minds, with 'every kind of wickedness' perverting their spirits and thus separating them from God. The teaching of the New Testament is that sin separates men and women from God and leads to spiritual death.

Paul saw his human nature as being 'unspiritual' and that he was 'sold as a slave to sin' which drove him to do things which he hated. He saw himself being driven by unseen forces of destruction which caused him to cry out, 'What a wretched man I am! Who will rescue me from this body of death?' But Paul was able to rejoice that 'through Christ Jesus the law of the Spirit of life set me free from the law of sin and death'. He realised that 'those controlled by the sinful nature cannot please God'. But those who have accepted Christ are not controlled by the sinful nature but by the Spirit of the living God (Rom 7:14–8:9).

The New Testament, through the teaching of Jesus and the apostles, affirms the values of the kingdom based upon the nature of God as originally revealed through the prophets under the Old Covenant. These are the values of *constancy*, *love*, *mercy*, *justice*, *holiness*, *faithfulness* and *truth*.

Upon these values the norms of a righteous and healthy society are based, which support happy and stable relationships within the family and community and enable individuals to find fulfilment through exercising their gifts and abilities within an acceptable and accepting social structure. A society having these values as its foundation will be a society in which behaviour is derived from norms which in turn are based upon fundamental values. Those values exclude greed, exploitation, oppression, injustice, idolatry, violence, murder, immorality and all the standards of behaviour which characterise sinful men and women who have rejected the word of God and are driven by their own evil desires which lead to both personal and communal destruction.

The teaching of the Bible is that the values of the kingdom of God are not only for the health of society but also for the happiness of each individual. That is God's desire for his children. He longs to see all his children in a right and loving relationship with him so that all things may work together for their good and his own good plans and purposes may be worked out in their lives as well as in the history of the nations. It is for this reason that God has revealed his own nature upon which the values of the kingdom are based. It was to establish the kingdom that Jesus came at his first advent. The message which Jesus himself declared and which he gave to his disciples was, 'The kingdom of God is here; it is already among you!' All those who believe enter the kingdom and embrace its values.

11

Re-establishing the Foundations

Nehemiah wept when he heard of the sorry condition of the remnant of the people living in Judah and that Jerusalem still lay in ruins with its walls broken down, its gates burned with fire and its once great buildings heaps of rubble so that all who passed by poured scorn upon the city and the name of its God. Nehemiah held a comfortable and secure post in the service of the King of Persia but his family ties remained strong and he remembered the covenant God had made with his forefathers. He records, 'When I heard these things, I sat down and wept. For some days I mourned and fasted and prayed' (Neh 1:4). But Nehemiah did not only grieve, fast and pray. His prayer led him to action. He risked everything in asking the king's permission to return to the land of his fathers and to rebuild the city which could become a potential threat to the security of the Persian Empire in the west.

Nehemiah had a vision for rebuilding the city and re-establishing the life of the nation. On his return to Jerusalem he shared this with the leaders of the community who also caught the vision and together they set about the task of reconstruction. They succeeded in accomplishing what appeared to be a hopeless project because, as Nehemiah recorded, 'The people worked with all their heart' (4:6).

The story of the reconstruction of Jerusalem under Nehemiah's leadership is a thrilling account of what can be achieved when a whole community embraces a shared vision. To anyone in Britain who is old enough to have witnessed the far-reaching changes which have taken place since the 1960s and the way in which the nation has turned away from its moral and spiritual heritage, the task of stemming the tide of social decay and re-establishing firm values must seem an impossibility. Indeed, humanly speaking it is an impossibility! But there *is* hope! That is what we intend to explore in these final chapters.

In some ways Nehemiah had the easier task because the destruction of the city was already complete, whereas the destructive forces are still at work in Britain and throughout the world today. As we have attempted to show in Chapter 3, the socio-economic forces in the modern world are highly complex. The truth of the statement 'No man is an island' has been widened in the second half of the twentieth century to apply to whole nations. No *nation* can be an island today, as Britain has discovered in her relationship with Europe. Even her physical separation has been broken down with the opening of the Channel Tunnel. The winds of change sweeping across the world are global rather than regional and they are increasing in velocity and ferocity as we approach the end of the second millennium and contemplate the awesome unknown of the twenty-first century.

The question in many people's minds is, 'How far into the third millennium will we get before the disintegrating forces of moral and spiritual decay will bring about a collapse of either the social order, or the economic structure, or both?'

Any attempt to answer this question takes us into the realm of speculation. There are so many variables!

(1) The present massive growth in world population—will it continue, or will it be checked by disease, plague or famine?

(2) The pollution of the environment through the expansion of industry and the massive growth of cities—will it continue, or can it be checked?

(3) The changes in the climate and global warming—how quickly will they progress?

(4) The incredible advances in technology over the past fifty years—will they continue and where will they lead?

(5) The growth of multi-national corporations in the past two or three decades, widening the gap between rich and poor and concentrating wealth in the hands of fewer and fewer people—will this end in the concentration of global power into the hands of a world dictator?

(6) The rising tide of violence and the spread of weapons of destruction—will these lead to global conflict?

These and many more unknowns are dark clouds on the world horizon making it impossible to predict the future on any rational or sociological basis. The very existence of these questions, however, underlines the significance of the days in which we live because of their similarity to biblical eschatology—that is, the picture presented in the Bible of events leading up to the end of the age. It is no part of our present purpose to examine this biblical literature. It is, however, an integral part of the theme of this book to recognise that there is both meaning and purpose in history and that what we are seeing today is not simply part of a random or cyclical pattern of events but rather a stage in the working out of the purposes of God in the history of the nations. That is the overarching theme running through this book. There are several propositions of immense significance which we have been endeavouring to establish. They are:

(1) The rapid and radical changes which have been taking place with gathering momentum throughout the twentieth century are driving the nations towards self-destruction.

(2) These forces of change are irreversible and unstoppable by any human effort. They are beyond the capacity of any single nation to control because modern technology and communications, plus the global nature of the economy, have bound the nations together in such a manner that they face a common destiny.

(3) The forces of change are so powerful that they have totally transformed every part of the world. There is hardly a people group left anywhere in the remotest regions of the world that has been left untouched by the changes sweeping across the world during this century.

(4) These changes have been so fundamental that they have disturbed the value system underlying each of the nations. Thus the foundations of the nations have been shaken. This has produced the equivalent of a social earthquake which has shaken the social structure and stability of most societies and has precipitated revolutionary social, political and economic changes which have left many nations reeling like a drunken man not knowing where they are going or what the future holds.

(5) We have attempted to establish the case for firmly rooted principles to re-establish the value system of the nations. It is our contention that the social values of a nation are rooted in its beliefs. It therefore

becomes essential that there should be clear teaching on the nature and purposes of God.

(6) We believe that the only source of truth about God is to be found in the biblical revelation which he began through the prophets of Israel and completed in the life, death and resurrection of the Lord Jesus Christ.

(7) Finally, it is our belief that only through the establishment of foundational values based upon biblical principles is there any hope of stemming the tide of disintegrating forces which are driving the nations towards destruction.

Our central concern in this book is to look at the situation in Britain, but due to the global nature of the social forces at work in the modern world we have been noting the international situation. Despite these global forces in the economy, in political affairs and in social and religious influences, there are things that individual nations can do to stem the tide of corruption and social disintegration sweeping across the world.

There have been other periods in our history when the nation has been in grave danger, such as at the beginning of the nineteenth century when there was widespread social unrest and the strong possibility of a revolution occurring in Britain similar to that of the French. The situation was compounded by poverty and distress among working people, the wide gap between rich and poor, a strong sense of injustice and exploitation of the weak by the powerful and widespread corruption at all levels of society.

In the first half of the nineteenth century two things of significance began to happen which clearly were the work of the Holy Spirit in the lives of believers. The first was the deep concern about the state of the nation and a compassion for those who were suffering; and secondly there was a turning to prayer and searching the Scriptures for biblically based policies of social, moral and spiritual renewal. It was in the early days of the century that the Clapham Sect was formed—the group of evangelicals whose numbers included men like Wilberforce and Shaftesbury—who were not only concerned to declare a full gospel of salvation in Jesus only, but also to work tirelessly for social justice through radical political reform.

There is a great need for a similar movement today which is both prayer-centred and biblically based. These are the essential characteristics of a prophetic movement which lays the foundation for national recovery. It was the dedicated witness of the reforming evangelicals which prepared the way for the revival which swept through England in the middle of the nineteenth century.

A most urgent need today is for the church to recover its confidence in the authority of the word of God so that insight and understanding can be given to the nation regarding the reasons for the stress and suffering being experienced by millions of people today. It has always been the task of the prophets to give such an understanding of the condition of the nation.

From the period of the Judges God always sent prophets in times of crisis to explain why things had gone wrong in the life of the nation and to point the way to healthier and more prosperous times. For example, in Judges 6 we read of Israel suffering under the invasion of large numbers of Midianites and Amalekites who were stripping the land of crops, sheep and cattle from one end of the country to the other.

In verse 7 it is recorded, 'When the Israelites cried to the Lord because of Midian, he sent them a prophet, who said, "This is what the Lord, the God of Israel, says . . . I said to you, 'I am the Lord your God; do not worship the gods of the Amorites, in whose land you live.' But you have not listened to me."' The prophet's task was to point to the spiritual reason for the social disorder. The account in Judges 6 also records the solution provided through the leadership of Gideon whose first task was to clear out the idolatry from his own family and clan, then to mobilise the people to drive out the enemy.

The church as the prophet to the nation has the responsibility for declaring that the fundamental reason why the present social conditions have been created which have led to so much personal suffering is that we have abandoned biblical standards in personal and social morality.

The method adopted by the prophets was always to remind the people of their heritage. An outstanding example of this occurred in the period we referred to at the beginning of this chapter. It was the time of the proclaimed resettlement of Judah following the exile in Babylon. Under the influence of Haggai the prophet, the city of Jerusalem, which had been totally destroyed by the Babylonians, gradually came back to life. Houses were built among the ruins, an altar was rebuilt on Mount Zion, and right worship reinstituted. Then the foundations of the Temple were relaid and over a period, despite much opposition, the second Temple was built. Some time later, during this period of reconstruction, Nehemiah obtained permission to rebuild the walls of Jerusalem and people from the various clans volunteered to live in the city and help rebuild its commercial and social life.

An important step in restoring the life of the nation was the re-establishing of moral and spiritual principles as the foundational values of the nation. This was done through the calling of a national assembly where Ezra the priest read from the Law and the Levites explained it to the people. 'They read from the book of the Law of God, making it clear and giving the meaning so that the people could understand what was being read' (Neh 8:8). Many of the people wept when they realised the reason for the series of disasters which had befallen the nation but they were told to stop grieving and to rejoice because God was now restoring the life of the nation.

After a short interval representatives from all the families and clans in Israel came together in Jerusalem. There was a strong emphasis upon confession and repentance. The record in Nehemiah 9:2 says, 'They stood in their places and confessed their sins and the wickedness of their fathers. They stood where they were and read from the book of the Law of the Lord their God for a quarter of the day, and spent another quarter in confession and in worshipping the Lord their God.' Thus confession was linked with the reading of the word of God and worship. This was followed by a long recital of the history of the nation going right back to the time of Abraham and linking the fortunes and misfortunes in different periods of their history with the faithfulness or unfaithfulness of their forefathers.

The passage in Nehemiah 9:25–37 is highly significant. It illustrates Hebrew thinking in regard to the sovereignty of God, his mercy and compassion linked with his power to control and use even unbelieving nations in order to work out his own purposes:

When they were oppressed they cried out to you. From heaven you heard them, and in your great compassion you gave them deliverers, who rescued them from the hand of their enemies. But as soon as they were at rest they again did what was evil in your sight. Then you abandoned them to the hand of their enemies so that they ruled over them. And when they cried out to you again, you heard from heaven, and in your compassion you delivered them time after time (vv 27–28).

This review of the history of the nation did two things of great importance. First, it taught the lessons to be learned from history. It underlined the need to heed the word of God, to remain faithful to him and not to be tempted to follow the ways of the world, ie the unbelieving peoples around them, not only in foreign nations, but those who lived in the land alongside them. In order to enjoy the blessings of God, which were part of the covenant relationship between God and the people, they had to remain faithful to the terms of the covenant.

Secondly, in reviewing the history of the nation the eyes of the people were focused upon the power of God, his sovereign control over all the nations and that he is the Creator of all things in the heavens and upon earth. He has the power to bless or to withhold blessing, but above all he is a God who is faithful to keep his promises to those who trust him and are faithful to him.

Here, then, is a biblical model of great importance for the situation facing all the nations in the western world today who have had centuries of biblical tradition in their heritage. Looking at the British situation we can observe that we are a nation that has openly declared to the world that we believe the word of God, and we acknowledge the Judeo-Christian heritage to be our heritage. Our major institutions of law and government are founded upon the word of God and our monarchy, as representative of the people, has for centuries been pledged through the Coronation Oath to uphold and maintain the faith.

The church is both priest and prophet to the nation. The priest speaks to God on behalf of the people and the prophet speaks to the people on behalf of God. In the time of Ezra and Nehemiah priest and prophet combined in calling a solemn assembly of representatives of the people to hear portions of the word of God. If we follow that model such an assembly would not only hear portions from both Old and New Testaments but would also hear a review of the nation's history.

The rebuilding of the foundations of the nation is neither a quick nor an easy task. Indeed, as in the physical world it is easier to break down and to destroy rather than to reconstruct, so the same is true in terms of re-laying moral and spiritual principles in the life of the nation. It has been our contention in this book that the moral and spiritual values which form the foundations of the social fabric of a nation are rooted in its beliefs. Thus the primary task in restoring the social order where that is disintegrating, as is clearly the case in Britain today, is to give highest priority to the beliefs of the nation.

It was the beliefs of the nation which changed radically in the 1960s under the combined impact of the rise of the pop culture, the decline in church attendance, the closure of Sunday schools and the neglect of teaching the Bible in day schools. As belief in God and knowledge of the word of God declined, the values of the nation changed rapidly. We have noted how these were reflected in the legislation of the day and in the changes in the behaviour of the nation, its family life, moral standards in honesty, integrity, justice and faithfulness. All of these have been reflected and promoted in the media.

Once we understand this process and the primacy of beliefs in regulating the behaviour of the nation the road to recovery becomes clear. We are then released from the bondage of fear to seek, under the guidance of the Holy Spirit, creative policies which will lead to the social and economic health and well-being of the nation.

Essential elements in a programme of rebuilding national, moral and spiritual foundations would include the following:

(1) A re-examination of the national heritage.
(2) A re-examination of the Judeo-Christian roots of the faith.

(3) A realistic assessment of current ethical standards in the life of the nation.

(4) A willingness to bring principles and practice into line with biblical standards.

(5) A re-affirmation of biblical faith as the foundational belief of the nation.

(6) An educational programme to teach all ages, especially the young, the basis of discipleship in line with New Testament teaching.

(7) A political programme of radical change to curb the excesses of behaviour which are out of line with biblical standards, such as the control of greed and corruption in the economy, injustice in social relationships and obscenity in the media.

(8) Measures to enlist the co-operation of the mass media in ensuring agreed standards in reporting and entertainment.

(9) A renewed and prayer-centred church in which biblical standards in the lifestyle of leaders are required and in the lives of committed believers are the expectation.

(10) A prophetic church, radically different from the world, seeking to listen to God, to understand his word and his ways, seeking only to do his will, to declare his word and to uphold the honour of his name.

The Ezra/Nehemiah model of re-establishing beliefs and values in the life of the nation included a review of the national heritage and history. This is an essential element if lessons are to be learned from history but it represents a major stumbling-block for the British. We have not only abandoned our moral and spiritual heritage, we have also turned our back upon our history. Nobody wants to talk about the British Empire and it is no longer even fashionable to speak about the British Commonwealth. We are ashamed of our history and most people simply want to forget it.

By contrast, although there were many things in Israel's past which made people feel ashamed, the prophets would never let them forget their history. They saw it as essential to remember and review events in the context of belief in the 'God of history' who is the God of all creation and who has the power and authority over all nations to work out his purposes. It is this belief in the God of history which has been lost not only in the nation but also in the church.

We have come back to this point a number of times throughout this book because it is of supreme importance in re-establishing biblically based beliefs in the nation. The God of the Bible is active in the affairs of all the nations and he is especially active among people who acknowledge his name. The promise given to Solomon at the dedication of the Temple held for all time: 'If my people, who are called by my Name, will humble them-selves and pray and seek my face and turn from their wicked ways, then I will hear from heaven and will forgive their sin and will heal their land' (2 Chron 7:14).

It is often objected that this promise was given to a nation in a covenant relationship with God. But it is the teaching of the apostles that such promises given to Israel are extended to those who enter into a covenant relation-ship with God through the blood of Christ. This does not mean that the church has replaced Israel but rather that God has established a new basis of the covenant through the Lord Jesus Christ into which both Jew and Gentile may freely enter, through faith in Jesus, as of equal status and brothers in Christ. As Paul puts it in Ephesians 2:14f, Christ has 'destroyed the barrier, the dividing wall of hostility' between Jew and Gentile. 'His purpose was to create in himself one new man out of the two . . . to reconcile both of them to God through the cross.' It is this one new man that is the true church of God and is composed of people of all races and nationalities who have come into a new relationship with God and with each other through faith in Jesus.

It is therefore with confidence that we can take the promise given to Solomon and apply it to our own situation. God is not waiting for the whole British nation, most of whom do not acknowledge him, to turn to him before he will bless them. The promise is addressed to those who are the people of God and who do acknowledge his name. In the British situation, if believers were collectively to stand upon that promise and seize the initiative, the impact upon the life of the nation would be immeasurable.

If in Britain we were prepared to review our national history we should see many things of which we may be justly proud as well as things of which to be ashamed. A great deal of good was achieved in going to other nations but harm was also done through greed and exploitation. We need to face these things honestly before God, seeing both the good and the evil, recognising where God has blessed the nation richly in times past and where things went wrong when the nation turned away from biblical principles and allowed greed, corruption, injustice and exploitation to become the driving force. Until we face these things honestly rather than shutting them up in a sealed mausoleum never to be exposed to public view, we shall never reach a position where right relationships between the nation and God can be restored.

God has already declared the strategy he would use in the closing days of the age to bring about a great turning of the nations to himself. This is seen as a mighty spiritual harvest that will be the prelude to the return of Jesus and the establishing of new heavens and a new earth as was first foreseen by the prophets and recorded in Isaiah 65:17. That strategy, foretold in Haggai 2:6–7 and repeated in Hebrews 12:26, is, as we have already stated, to shake all things both in the natural creation and in the social, economic and political institutions of the nations. The events which we are witnessing in the world today bear remarkable similarity to these prophecies.

In Britain the shaking of the nation has been having a profound effect upon the lives of millions of people through unemployment, through the breakdown of family life, through crime and disorder, through child abuse and violence and through the general effect of the rapid changes in society which have had such a disturbing effect and produced high levels of stress in most people throughout the nation.

The point is not far away where many people in Britain will have been so shaken by the experiences of stress and suffering that they will be open to the gospel. It is at this point that the prophetic declaration of the word of God becomes acceptable as it gives explanation of what has gone wrong in individual lives and in the life of the nation.

At the time of writing there are no signs of revival in Britain. But it may not be long before the shaking of the nation creates a new openness to the gospel and people are ready to give a hearing to the biblical word of God and to turn away from the paths that are leading to social and economic disaster. There are many who have grown weary of the failed policies and broken promises of a materialistic acquisitive society and are prepared to look for new ways, just as the men of violence in Northern Ireland eventually grew tired of the ways of violence and murder and began to look for other ways to achieve their objectives. That does not mean that people are ready to repent any more than the men of violence in Ulster came to a sudden point of repentance. The point we are making is simply that people have grown weary of the old ways and the misery these have produced, and the day is drawing near when there will be openness to seek a new way. That is the opportunity which the shaking of the nations is creating. It is the opportunity for which the prophets in ancient Israel always looked. It is the opportunity for which the church, if we were sensitive to our prophetic mission, should be eagerly awaiting and seeking to grasp.

It is the responsibility of leaders in the church not only to understand the state of the nation, but also to discern God's strategy for bringing the nation to repentance and renewal of its moral and spiritual life. That repentance begins with the church, with the recognition of how far we have strayed from the paths of righteousness and the poor example we have given to the nation. The church bears a large measure of responsibility for the present state of the nation and when we confess this before God there will be a healing within the church and a release of the power of God. There are many biblical instances of this happening as, for example, in the time of Ezra and Nehemiah. They not only recognised the plight of the nation but also the responsibilities of its religious leaders. 'While Ezra was praying and confessing, weeping and throwing himself down before the house of God, a large crowd of Israelites—men, women and children—gathered round him. They too wept bitterly' (Ezra 10:1).

The key to recovery in Britain today lies in the spiritual sensitivity of leaders within the church. The greatest stumbling-block to revival is not the hardness of the nation or its spiritual apathy or moral decadence. The greatest stumbling-block to revival lies within the church itself! It is this situation which we will address in the final chapter.

12

A Future and a Hope

This is the plight of the world—the nations are being driven by unstoppable forces. The winds of change are blowing with increasing fury across the world. They have presently reached storm force; soon they will be a hurricane. The genie is out of the bottle and the nations are unable to put it back. They are being driven by forces they are powerless to control.

We have reached a critical point in world history. The sinfulness of humanity which has been in the world since the Fall has succeeded in developing the technology, not only to destroy whole cities with weapons of mass destruction, or to wipe out large population groups with chemical or biological weapons, but actually to destroy all life on the planet. This is the fear which has gripped leaders of the nations throughout the second half of this century. As the twenty-first century looms closer there is a new fear occupying the attention of world leaders. It is the recognition that global forces affecting the balance of the natural order of creation are combining with social, economic and political forces to destabilise the world. Of particular concern are two sets of forces which are pulling in opposite directions.

In terms of social and economic forces, on the one hand there is a strong movement towards a global economy. The growth of multi-national corporations, the increasing

200

size and power of financial institutions, the elimination of competitors, the pressure to achieve a single European currency as a step towards a world currency, are all examples of the drive towards a one-world economy and power structure.

On the other hand a resurgence of nationalism and ethnic consciousness is creating social and political drives towards fragmentation. The 1990s have seen a proliferation of ethnic conflicts throughout the world. The break-up of the Soviet Union contributed to this and led to conflicts among the states of the former USSR and the bloodletting between Serb, Croat and Muslim in the former Yugoslavia. Additionally, Africa and the Indian sub-continents have seen a resurgence of tribal conflicts.

Thus economic and social forces are pulling in opposite directions, which can only lead to an increase in world tension and mounting chaos and conflict.

The second pair of opposite forces affect population and environment. On the one hand the world population continues to grow at an alarming rate, especially in the poorest nations. At the same time world grain production and food supplies are threatened by global pollution and environmental deterioration.

There are a number of other global forces at work in the world which are giving anxiety to world leaders. The biotech agricultural revolution and the computerised automation revolution in manufacturing and commerce is drastically reducing the manpower required to operate these systems. This is a direct threat to the lifestyle of millions of people in the rich nations where full employment is unlikely to be seen again in the foreseeable future.

The global economy means that multi-national corporations are finding it more profitable to build plants in third-world countries where labour is cheap, thus further reducing employment prospects in the rich industrial nations.

The outlook for the twenty-first century is bleak according to most analysts. There is general agreement that a crisis point will be reached sometime towards the middle of the century. Many secular observers believe that unless there are drastic changes in global policy the world cannot survive beyond about 2040 without experiencing some kind of massive catastrophe.

This gloomy forecast is in some ways in line with biblical eschatology. Certainly the global forces of change will increase pressure for the formation of a one-world government to control a one-world economy. We may also see the rise in ethnic conflict produce a demand for an enforced one-world religion. Thus the scenario envisaged in Revelation 13 would be complete.

Nevertheless, the difference between the secular and biblical viewpoints is extreme. In contrast to the Utopianism with which the world entered the twentieth century the nations are going forward into the twenty-first with a sense of hopelessness and despair. The only hope they recognise lies in global human action. But this is the very policy which will produce the great dictator prophesied in Revelation—the one hailed as a saviour who will enslave the nations.

By contrast the biblical viewpoint is one of hope in the midst of chaos. The biblical prophets and the teaching of Jesus point to the God of history still being in control and working his purposes out despite the clamour, confusion and violence of the nations. In fact Jesus said we should rejoice when things begin to get really bad as this is a sign that the day of liberation draws near.

The global world situation is beginning to show the signs Jesus referred to in Matthew 24. The enemy is orchestrating the forces of destruction which are sweeping across the world with ever-increasing momentum. Humanly speaking they are unstoppable. Only God has the power to overcome them. Where are the prophets to declare the word of the living God to the nations today? Where are the prophetic voices that will be heard above the clamour of the sirens of the New Age, the mullahs of Islam and the secular humanist politicians?

God has already provided the prophet to the nations through the working of the Holy Spirit within the church which has been gathering momentum throughout the twentieth century. Since the beginning of the century God has been active in his church in a new way, reviving, renewing and refreshing his people, breaking down barriers between denominations, giving mighty spiritual awakenings in lands where the gospel was unknown in previous centuries. The reason why God is arming his church with the power of his Holy Spirit to be used under the discipline and tutelage of the word of God is in order to raise up a people able to withstand the onslaught of the enemy in these days.

But the church is not ready for battle because its leaders have failed to understand the signs of the times. They have failed to grasp the reasons why God has been giving a mighty outpouring of the Holy Spirit through this century. Instead of receiving the Spirit with joy and humility and coming before God with reverence and awe to seek to understand his ways and his purposes in the contemporary world and what he is requiring of his church, many leaders in the churches have set their faces against receiving the Holy Spirit. Others have seized the gifts of the Spirit with worldly hands for their own enjoyment or self-aggrandisement.

The greatest danger facing the world today is the weakness of the church in the western nations at the most critical period of world history for 2,000 years. Even secular 'prophets' are warning that the path along which the nations of the world are heading can only lead to disaster. But they can only give warnings—they do not have the answers. Such answers as they offer do not go to the root causes of the present plight of the world. Only the word of God does that.

The church in Europe and the western industrialised nations is numerically weaker at the end of the twentieth century than at the beginning. It is significantly weaker in terms of percentage of population in regular church attendance, and immeasurably weaker in terms of social significance. But that is not the real weakness of the church. God has never carried out his saving purposes by strength of numbers. The real weakness of the church lies in its loss of confidence in biblical truth. A major consequence of this has been the losing sight of the God of history; the recognition that God is active in human affairs and the failure to understand the great significance within the purposes of God of what is happening in the world today. The result is that the church is unable to interpret contemporary history. It is unable to declare the contemporary word of the contemporary God to the contemporary world.

It may be that within the purposes of God he will bypass the western churches and raise up prophets from the poorer nations so often despised by the rich nations. The church in Asia, Africa and South America is growing at an incredible pace and the faith of believers in these nations is dynamic. Lacking the sophistication of western theological education and lacking the vast material resources available to western Christians, believers in the poorer nations simply believe the Bible and have no alternative but to trust God for everything in their lives. Many of them face fierce opposition and persecution even unto death.

Since 1990 the annual figures for martyrs, those believers who have lost their lives for the sake of the gospel, has exceeded 300,000. It may be that God will use the vibrant faith of believers in the newest churches of the poorest nations to carry out his purposes of salvation in the world.

This indeed would be fully in accord with biblical principles and the way God has acted in times past. Mary, the mother of Jesus, when told that she was to be the mother of the Redeemer, rejoiced in the vision she saw of God putting down the rich and worldly powerful and raising up the poor and spiritually powerful.

There is, however, still hope for the church in the West if those who are committed Christians would but open their eyes and see what is happening in the world and read the Scriptures with fresh understanding. The church in the West (of all denominations) is suffering from a form of spiritual myopia, that is, a short-sightedness that produces blindness to the significance of events on the world scene.

This myopic condition affects churches of all types. The churches in the West can broadly be classified under three categories: the *traditionalists*, the *liberals* and the *evangelicals*.

The *traditionalists*, which includes most of the Catholic and Episcopal churches, are so committed to following tradition and carrying out the routine of religious practice that they have little awareness of the changing world around them. This, for centuries, produced an attitude of apathy and complacency. Today, under the stress of the forces of change sweeping across the world, it is producing an attitude of defiant conservatism; a 'head-in-the-sand' attitude which refuses to acknowledge the onslaughts of the enemy, but which also, for many, shuts out the Spirit of the living God.

The *liberal* churches, with their emphasis upon critical biblical scholarship, often compensate for the lack of personal experience of God and the lack of belief in a God of salvation by a strong commitment to social action. This often results in espousing many worthy causes and serving the community with selfless devotion and great commitment. Such service is honouring to God and a good witness to his love but it produces a blindness to the activity of God in the world. Most liberal churches are not only closed to the Holy Spirit but their lack of confidence in the Bible as the word of God blinds them to an understanding of the God of history and to his activity in the world today.

The *evangelical* churches, which include the Pentecostal and charismatic fellowships, with their commitment to preaching a gospel of personal salvation, are prone to lose sight of the macro purposes of God and become locked into an individualistic gospel. Yet it is within these churches that there lies a real hope of the voice of the prophet being heard among the nations. It is this sector of the church that is not locked in to tradition—indeed, it is only too open for anything fresh and new! Neither is it blinded by the unbelief of critical liberal scholarship that has emasculated the authority of Scripture.

Unlike the rest of the church, evangelicals are generally aware of the biblical significance of the times in which we live. Indeed, among many evangelicals there is an obsession with the mechanical use of biblical prophecy concerning the end times and the literal interpretation of apocalyptic scriptures. Others go to elaborate lengths to produce charts and timetables attempting to predict the date of the *parousia* or the battle of Amageddon and the end of the world. These studies divert attention from the purposes of God for his church today.

Another attractive diversion which blinds many evangelicals to the purposes of God for his church today is the belief in the pre-tribulation Rapture. By this means many evangelicals believe they will escape from the world before anything disastrous occurs. Such a belief fails to recognise that throughout the biblical record of God's dealings with his people he has always used suffering in a redemptive manner. The cross is at the very heart of the gospel. The God who did not spare his own Son but delivered him up for us all, and who did not spare the apostles and saints of the early church from suffering and martyrdom, is hardly likely to change his ways for the comfort of twentieth-century materialistic worldly believers.

The church throughout the western nations has made friends with the world. Hosea made reference to this in the spiritual life of Israel in a telling phrase, 'Ephraim mixes with the nations . . . foreigners sap his strength but he does not realise it. His hair is sprinkled with grey but he does not notice' (6:8–9). Hosea meant that the days of the nation were numbered, disaster was close because the door to the world had been opened wide, but the people were unaware of the danger. There is a parallel with many parts of the church today.

In Britain the mainline churches are still suffering from a massive overdose of institutionalisation and liberal theology. The combined effects have destroyed vision, blunted mission and caused spiritual blindness and deafness which in turn have produced dumbness—an inability to declare the word of God with power and authority. Weak inept leadership combined with a lack of confidence in the Bible as the word of God has resulted in a lack of vibrant faith, a mindset adjusted to decline and powerlessness and a lack of belief in the power or ability of God to fulfil his promises. For most of the second half of the century the mainline churches have been content to play the role of maintaining traditional religion, making the occasional foray into social and political affairs but lacking any concept of propetic mission or spiritual empowering from an omnipotent God.

It is out of this cradle of unbelief and spiritual atrophy that the charismatic renewal movement and the new independent fellowships were born. The charismatic movement has brought new life and vitality to churches of all denominations throughout the UK. It has brought new hymns and Scripture-based songs of praise and the use of many different instruments, breaking the monopoly of the pipe organ. This has had a transforming effect upon the worship of millions of believers. It has also been responsible for breaking the monopoly of the priest and professional minister in matters religious.

The renewed emphasis upon spiritual gifts as recorded in the New Testament and regularly practised in the early church has enabled lay people to play a significant part not only in praise and worship, but also in many other spheres of ministry. Yet this emphasis upon the availability of spiritual gifts through the Holy Spirit in the lives of all believers, which has broken the mould of the ordained ministry, has also been responsible to a large degree for the 'me-centredness' of charismatic teaching and practice.

This emphasis upon the needs and personal experience of each individual believer is an understandable swing of the pendulum away from the impersonal religion of the traditional ordained clergy-dominated churches. But there are strong indications that the pendulum has swung too far. Although some charismatic fellowships are involved in evangelistic outreach and in social programmes serving the needs of their local communities, many fellowships limit their activities to teaching and ministering to the needs of their own members. In these days when levels of stress in most people's lives are high, many churches are stretched to meet these internal pastoral needs and have little time or energy for outreach or the care of others outside the church.

This inward-looking orientation has been encouraged by various strands within the charismatic movement. The faith and prosperity teachers, for example, place considerable stress upon faith being the key to meeting the physical needs of each individual. They teach that to speak the word of faith into a situation releases creative spiritual energy which accomplishes that which is desired. This is dangerously close to New Age teaching! The faith teachers say that God wants us all to be healthy and prosperous; lack of prosperity or ill-health are the results of the activity of Satan. This is not only a distortion of biblical teaching, which rules out the possibility of redemptive suffering including the cross at the heart of the gospel, but it places an unhealthy emphasis upon the value of physical things. It contributes to the me-centred individualism of many charismatic fellowships, which is more a reflection of the world than of the Spirit of Jesus.

In fact the emphasis upon health and prosperity is precisely in line with that of western culture in the rich industrialised nations. The faith and prosperity teachers usually make use of the Bible by taking selective texts and quoting them in support of their theories rather than deriving their teaching from the context of the Scriptures themselves. Numerous examples could be given but this is not the place to undertake such a critique of these teachings, and the literature on this subject is already quite extensive. Our purpose in referring to these distortions of biblical truth is simply to indicate the extent to which the values of the world have permeated even those sectors of the church in the western nations which claim to be directed by the power and authority of the Holy Spirit.

There is abundant evidence that the values of the world have penetrated churches of all traditions today. The much publicised moral failings of the clergy and leaders in all sections of the church no longer shock the world; they simply increase its scorn. Marriage breakdown, homosexuality and scandals are commonplace in the church of the late twentieth century. These have blunted the church's witness and brought dishonour to the name of Christ. There is also abundant evidence that the New Age has penetrated the church. All kinds of strange spiritual phenomena being peddled as part of the church's programme.

This underlines the weakness of the church in the

western nations which has made friends with the world. But by far the greatest irony of the present situation is the fact that it is many of those who have responded to God through the present-day working of the Holy Spirit who are foremost in having made friends with the world. Many leaders within the charismatic movement have been caught up in wave after wave of excitement like little children let loose in a toy shop trying to lay their hands on everything their eyes see. It's 'Give me this' and 'Give me that!' Just as the world values power, authority and status, many charismatics have coveted these things. Just as the world values personal wealth, comfort, security and health, many charismatics have coveted all these things.

The rise of the Latter Rain teachings in the aftermath of World War Two has given rise to the present Restorationist teachings implicit in large sectors of the charismatic movement today. These teachings were branded heretical by the Assemblies of God in Canada in 1949 but they have persisted in one form or another. Most charismatics have no understanding of the subtle links between Dominionism and Restoration theology and the teachings of New Agers which go right back to first-century Gnosticism which was declared heretical by the early church.

Like Gnosticism and New Age teaching, Dominionism promises the believer divine power and authority—power to exercise dominion over the nations and over the whole created order. It is a subtle form of deception that has crept into the teachings of many of the well-known and popular charismatic leaders. It has subtly entered the minds of the people through many of the songs and choruses sung with uncritical simplicity by millions of charismatics who love to think of themselves as rising like a mighty army to march upon the land and to subdue the nations, trampling upon the enemies of the gospel and rejoicing in their power to triumph victoriously over all opposition!

Popular 'Manifest Sons of God' teaching, which grew out of the Latter Rain movement, has penetrated even the mainline charismatic churches who see present-day believers or their children as being part of the end-time generation who will possess a power greater than that known by the apostles or the New Testament church because God is empowering the saints to do mighty exploits and to establish the kingdom on earth now. They believe that when all is ready Christ will return to reign with his church on earth. One dangerous conclusion of this teaching could be that it is the modern-day saints who gain all the glory for subduing the enemies of the gospel rather than Christ who returns when the believers have done the work and are ready to present the kingdom to him. Many sincere believers with an inadequate knowledge of the Bible may fail to discern the subtleties with which these teachings are presented by well-known leaders whom they revere.

It is tragic that in the closing decades of the second millennium, when God is renewing his covenant with his church after centuries of clericalism, the subtleties of deception are abounding to distract believers from the central purposes of God. Instead of being transformed into the church militant, a prepared and an obedient people, the church is being transformed from the 'church dormant' to the 'church heretical'. It is a church that goes about its business in ways that are indistinguishable from those of the world.

It is God's intention in these days to empower his church with the Holy Spirit giving gifts to all believers, thus liberating them from the deadening effects of clericalism into the liberty of a Spirit-filled body of believers. But there is a new danger today through preachers who enjoy the adulation of the people as they entertain the multitudes with promises of power and spectacular demonstrations of signs and wonders.

Their policies are often pragmatic—if it works it's true! Many people are excited to attend large celebration events, where the emphasis is upon experience. These meetings are often advertised as 'come and experience the power!' rather than as an opportunity to hear the word of God. But an experiential faith needs regular topping up. It acts like a drug to help people forget the harsh realities of the world around them and to live in a kind of fantasy world. But it is a world that quickly fades and its worshippers require a fresh 'shot-in-the-arm' before disappointment, disillusionment and depression set in to dispel shallow faith. So the PA is turned up a few more decibels, the 'ad' men go to work to present more attractive programmes, the preachers bring fresh exciting teachings, the prophets give new sensational promises and the people love it! It is just as it was in Jeremiah's day: 'A horrible and shocking thing has happened in the land; the prophets prophesy lies, the priests rule by their own authority, and my people love it this way,' but Jeremiah adds with penetrating insight, 'But what will you do in the end?' (5:30–31).

That is the question! 'What will you do in the end?' What will these preachers and prophets do who are deceived, if not deceivers? What will the people do who have been deceived? Each one of us is accountable before God for our lives and for our stewardship of spiritual gifts, for our handling of the word of God. The principle of accountability is that 'unto whomsoever much is given of him shall be much required' (Lk 12:48, AV). Those who have great influence also have great responsibility and will one day have to give account before God of their ministries. None of us needs to be deceived, even the humblest believer, for each of us has access to the truth. Jeremiah 31:31 speaks of the time coming when God would establish a New Covenant relationship with his people which would enable each one to know him for themselves. That New Covenant would be written on the heart and not simply upon tablets of stone. The New Covenant has been established through the precious blood of the Lord Jesus Christ who gave himself for us. We have been redeemed from the world through Christ and brought into a right relationship with the living God who has given us his word. He expects us to study that word which enables us to understand his very nature and purposes and thereby to understand his activity in the world.

Jesus spoke severely to the crowds in Jerusalem who had the word of God and the teaching of the Torah and the prophets but failed to understand the times in which they lived. He said, 'When you see a cloud rising in the west, immediately you say, "It's going to rain," and it does. And when the south wind blows, you say, "It's going to be hot," and it is. Hypocrites! You know how to interpret the appearance of the earth and the sky. How is it that you don't know how to interpret this present time?' (Lk 12:54–56).

If Jesus was so stern in warning the people of Jerusalem of the consequences of their hardness of heart and their blindness in failing to understand the signs of the times, how much more does he expect of us who have believed his testimony and accepted him as our Lord and Saviour? We, who claim to be the people of the New Covenant, have been entrusted with the precious word of life, the gospel of salvation, the knowledge of him who is the way, the truth and the life and who is the only source of light in the darkness of the world.

There is no excuse for being deceived, because we have access to the truth. We can check out the teachings of those who claim to be interpreters of the word or to be bringing new teachings, new revelations or new interpretations. We should never simply accept them uncritically, however attractive they may appear to be.

I was recently leading an In-Service training course for clergy and ministers from different denominations. We were considering the rise of the New Age movement in the late twentieth century and analysing some of its teachings. Leading the seminar was a believer who for some years had been immersed in the New Age movement before experiencing a dramatic conversion. It was mid-winter in England when flowers were scarce but on the table was a vase with a beautiful display of blooms. He asked the class if they were real or artificial. Immediately there was division. Some said, 'They're real!' Others said, 'No, they are artificial!' He then invited the class to come forward and examine them closely, to touch them and to smell them. Slowly the reality dawned—here was a mixture; some were real flowers, but mixed in among them were artificial leaves and blooms of high quality that looked real until they were examined closely.

This is a parable. There are two parallel forces driving through the church today. One is real, the other is counterfeit. One is the Holy Spirit, the other is a satanic alien spirit. The alien spirit, which may simply be a reflection of worldly values, is particularly attractive because it comes with excitement, with promises of all good things and is neatly packaged in a way that especially appeals to twentieth-century believers moulded by the values of the world, desiring health and prosperity, power and glory, excitement and fulfilling experiences. These are so much more attractive than repentance and humility which lead to love, joy, peace, patience, kindness, goodness, faithfulness, gentleness and self-control, which Paul says are the fruit of the Holy Spirit (Gal 5:22).

During the past two decades the charismatic movement has produced wave after wave of fresh emphases, each with a strong experiential basis. There was the emphasis upon praise from which emerged the first group of songs that began to transform worship. There was the emphasis upon tongues and everybody strove to speak in tongues and to give interpretations. Then the emphasis swung onto healing which generated a fresh wave of excitement drawing large crowds together to learn how to pray for the sick. There were many casualties of this wave as not everyone was healed and the sick were often accused of a lack of faith and those praying felt condemned.

Then came the wave which generated many conferences on spiritual warfare. Ley lines were studied, high places were visited, marches were organised and some strange teachings arose. This wave also produced many casualties as in some fellowships anyone sick was thought to be demonically possessed and those suffering from stress, depression or psychiatric disorders were targeted, often with disastrous results. Then came the wave of prophecy which spread like wildfire across some churches. Crowds flocked to big meetings to hear men who could seemingly pick out people from the crowd and give them a personal message straight from God.

These demonstrations of supernatural knowledge dazzled the crowds and lowered their resistance to false teaching. But the prophecy wave began to fade when the major prophecies proved to be false. In 1993 a new wave of manifestations began to appear in Florida and California and various other parts of the USA. Early in 1994 this spread to Toronto from where it leap-frogged into Britain and became known as the 'Toronto Blessing'. There were strange manifestations including making animal noises, falling around in a drunken stupor, uncontrollable body movements, laughter and weeping. At the same time there was evidence that God was blessing his people and many testified to a fresh experience of his presence and a deeper love for the Lord Jesus.

This new wave, however, exposed a fundamental

weakness in the charismatic movement which has tended to move popular teaching further away from its original biblical basis. The movement began with the study of Scripture and a renewed emphasis upon the exercise of spiritual gifts in the church of New Testament times. By the time the Toronto Blessing was reached the whole process had been reversed. Instead of practice flowing out of Scripture, Scripture was sought to justify practice. It was astonishing to read and hear the verses quoted by well-known preachers and teachers in justification of the strange phenomena occurring at the meetings they led. It was as though they reached for a concordance and looked up any reference relating to animal noises, drunkenness, falling down, laughter, and such, and simply quoted them regardless of context.

Many leaders declared that the Toronto Blessing was a time of spiritual refreshment which God was using to prepare his people for revival. These promises came from the same leaders who had promised a great revival four or five years earlier during the prophecy wave. But in fact each fresh wave within the charismatic movement for the past twenty years has been accompanied by promises of revival. Each one was said to be preparing the people so that they would be ready for the great national outpouring of the Holy Spirit. But each wave ended in disappointment as the promises of revival were never fulfilled.

In biblical times promises of revival always came from the false prophets. Jeremiah continually battled with them in an attempt to undo the harm they were doing by instilling a dangerous attitude of complacency among the people at a time of great danger. Many times Jeremiah had to say, 'Do not listen to what the prophets are prophesying to you; they fill you with false hopes. They speak visions from their own minds, not from the mouth of the Lord' (Jer 23:16). His complaint was that none of these false prophets had 'stood in the council of the Lord to see or hear his word' (v 18) and that if they had done so they would have proclaimed the word of God which would have turned the people away from their evil ways and saved them from the disaster which was coming upon them (v 22).

The record of prophecy throughout the Bible shows that God never sends prophets to foretell times of peace and prosperity. He raises up prophets in times of trouble to prepare the people to be able to withstand the difficult days that lie ahead, or to call them back to faithful trust in the Lord so that God can intervene and miraculously change the situation. In this way God gets all the glory for accomplishing something which was humanly impossible.

There are numerous examples in the Bible of such miraculous intervention. A notable God-given victory occurred during the reign of Jehoshaphat and is recorded in 2 Chronicles 20 when a vast army came against the tiny state of Judah. 'Alarmed, Jehoshapat resolved to enquire of the Lord, and he proclaimed a fast for all Judah. The people of Judah came together to seek help from the Lord' (v 3). Jehoshaphat led the people in a prayer, which is a model for approaching God during times of trouble, 'We have no power to face this vast army that is attacking us. We do not know what to do, but our eyes are upon you' (v 12). God responded through a prophet and gave them the strategy for facing the enemy, but it was God who achieved the victory and Jehoshaphat acknowledged this by leading the people to the Temple to praise God.

There is no record in the Bible of God ever sending prophets to prepare the people for revival or to foretell good times that lie ahead. The prophets are the watchmen of the people and their job is to give forewarning of danger, not to encourage excitement or contentment. There are instances where the message of warning and strong calls for repentance and change of behaviour resulted in revival, but this followed directly upon the warnings being heeded and the word of God being obeyed.

A good example of revival following strong words of warning occurred in the ministry of the prophet Isaiah who began by saying, 'Ah, sinful nation, a people loaded with guilt, a brood of evildoers, children given to corruption! They have forsaken the Lord; they have spurned the holy one of Israel and turned their backs on him' (Is 1:4)— strong words of condemnation. But the prophet went even further, saying that God hated the worship they were offering and would no longer listen to their prayers of intercession. 'Even if you offer many prayers, I will not listen' (vv 11–15). He warned of coming disaster but his words were heard and heeded and led to the great revival led by Hezekiah and the defeat of the Assyrian army which was threatening to destroy Jerusalem (Is 37:36).

Following repentance and revival Isaiah was instructed to change the message from warning of impending disaster to a promise that God would now defend Jerusalem and defeat the invading Assyrian army.

In Jeremiah's time both leaders and people refused to hear or heed the warnings, so the prophet was never able to change the message. In fact in the end he was told to stop interceding for the nation because it was too late.

Jeremiah had to tell those who were prophesying good news that God was against them and would hold them responsible for the harm they were doing to the people who believed their false prophecies. He came face to face with the prophet Hananiah who was foretelling revival and said, 'Listen, Hananiah! The Lord has not sent you, yet you have persuaded this nation to trust in lies' (Jer 28:15). Jeremiah based his conviction upon all that he knew of the role of the prophet. He said, 'From early times the prophets who preceded you and me have prophesied war, disaster and plague against many countries and great kingdoms. But the prophet who prophesies peace will be recognised as one truly sent by the Lord only if his prediction comes true' (Jer 28:8–9).

That basic biblical principle holds true today. Those who come with exciting messages of imminent revival and of a great outpouring of the Spirit of God in power upon his people but who are not first calling for repentance as a prerequisite are bringing false prophecies which are not from the Lord and they are doing immense harm among the people. That is not to deny that they are brothers in Christ, or that they love the Lord, but they have certainly got the message wrong, probably because they have not understood the times in which we live and therefore not got into the presence of the Lord with that understanding. Consequently they have not been able to receive the response of the Lord to what is happening in the contemporary world and the imminent danger facing us.

If leaders making these false promises of revival would only read the accounts of earlier revivals they would see some startling contrasts with the present situation which give some understanding of why genuine revival does not, and never will, flow out of the experiential waves of the charismatic movement.

The great revivals of the past two or three hundred years, such as the eighteenth-century Wesleyan revival, the nineteenth-century evangelical revival and the early twentieth-century Welsh revival, had a number of things in common. Notably, the preachers were convinced that unrepentant sinners were going to hell. Their preaching was full of persuasion and deep compassion. It was firmly based upon the word of God. As the Bible was read and expounded the people responded with penitence and tears of repentance, often falling down before the awesome majesty of God under the deep conviction of their own sinfulness. Former

generations of preachers spoke with such passionate elo-
quence that sinners could amost smell the fires of hell.

Today most preachers rarely mention hell and those
who do usually sanitise their pronouncements and present
things in a more polite and reasonable way considered to
be more appropriate to the sophisticated culture of late
twentieth-century western society. In contrast to the nineteenth century, many preachers are less motivated by a
deep sense of compassion for the millions going to a lost
eternity. Perhaps we are so saturated with scenes of horror
on film and TV and in news stories that we have become
hardened. Popular preachers tend to respond to modern
humanity's obsession with the supernatural and try to base
their appeal around spiritual phenomena. 'Come and witness the mighty demonstrations of supernatural power.'
This is the kind of invitation more likely to appeal to
people today, but it will not accomplish the will of the
Lord, which is to warn people of dangerous days ahead
and to call his people to a new obedience to him.

Revival will not come until there is repentance and the
faithful preaching of the word of God. In fact, if revival
did come as a result of the many strange supernatural
manifestations which have been seen at recent charismatic meetings, it could be a counterfeit revival! It could
be the result of people responding to a different Jesus, and
looking for a different kingdom.

There is a grave danger today of such a counterfeit
revival occurring in Britain which is a highly secular
post-Christian society with little or no knowledge of the
Bible but a fascination for the supernatural. A 1994 survey
revealed that Britain has 30,000 witches, which is more
than the number of ordained ministers serving churches.
Britain is a nation that has turned back to its pagan roots,
and vast numbers of people have been influenced by the
occult in some form or other.

Israel was a nation in a covenant relationship with God which has not been extended to any other nation. There are, nevertheless, lessons we can learn from the history of Israel which we can apply to Gentile nations, particularly those that have centuries of Christian heritage in their past. If a nation has once publicly acknowledged the God and Father of the Lord Jesus Christ to be its God and the Bible to be its rule of life, that nation voluntarily places itself in a special relationship to God. So long as the nation is faithful in honouring the word of the Lord and seeking to glorify the Lord Jesus in its national life, that nation will enjoy the blessing and protection of God. But if that nation turns away to worship other gods and spurns the word of the Lord, just as Israel did on many occasions, it brings judgement upon itself in the same way as national disaster came upon Israel.

It was in times of unfaithfulness that God raised up prophets in Israel to explain why things had gone wrong, to warn of coming danger and to call the people to return to the Lord and put their trust in him.

Britain and many other western nations have acknowledged God in former generations and have turned away from him in the twentieth century, so that today they are facing grave danger at the same time as a series of economic, political and social forces with immense destructive potential has been loosed in the world. We live in an age of increasing violence when aggressive tactics are adopted in many walks of secular life and commercial and industrial activity in order to achieve desired ends. We may expect to see increasing levels of international terrorism as well as the activity of fanatical religious cults that will terrorise whole populations similar to the fear in Tokyo following the poisoned gas attack in the Tokyo subway system in March 1995 and the fear in the USA following the Oklahoma bombing in April 1995.

God is arming his church for battle for the days that lie ahead. Through the power of his Holy Spirit he is strengthening his people to stand the test of violent opposition to the gospel and persecution of believers. At the same time he is calling upon his people to rise up and declare his word to the nations as did the prophets of old. The church in each nation is called to be the prophet to that nation. The people whom God has called out from every nation to be his people of the New Covenant, Jew and Gentile, through the redeeming work of Christ, are called to be a prophetic people in these times. They are the watchmen of the Lord called to pace the city walls and to declare his word from the housetops.

God has not yet told his prophets to stop praying for the nations as Jeremiah was told on three occasions (Jer 7:16; 11:14; 14:11). At the moment there is still hope. The word of the Lord is still a call to repentance and a plea to turn to him and be saved (Is 45:22). But the destructive spirit of lawlessness that is sweeping across the world and the forces of darkness which are driving the nations are gathering momentum.

Humanly speaking they are unstoppable. Only God can save the world. But he has entrusted the message of salvation to his church. He has given the power of his Holy Spirit to enable the mission to be accomplished. Will his church awake from her slumbers; will she throw off the shackles of unbelief; will she repent of her self-centredness before it becomes too late? At the moment there is still time, but it is fast running out.

May the God of history, who is working out his good purposes in the world today, open eyes that are blind among his own people, unstop ears that are deaf and loosen the tongues of his people to declare his word among the nations.